M000286734

STITCHING TOGETHER AN ESSAY

A GUIDE TO COLLEGE WRITING

BY
BRENDON ZATIRKA
CITY COLLEGES OF CHICAGO

cognella®
academic publishing

Bassim Hamadeh, CEO and Publisher
Michael Simpson, Vice President of Acquisitions and Sales
Jamie Giganti, Senior Managing Editor
Miguel Macias, Graphic Designer
Angela Schultz, Senior Field Acquisitions Editor
Michelle Piehl, Project Editor
Alexa Lucido, Licensing Coordinator
Rachel Singer, Interior Designer

www.cognella.com   800-200-3908

CONTENTS

To those with tired eyes,
unbending determination
and an unstoppable fire.

But why do I speak of all this? Not long
Ago, I, perchance, beheld a book,
Written with old letters;
And thereupon, a certain thing to learn,
I read so swiftly and fervently for the long day.

For out of old fields, as men say,
Come all this new corn from year to year,
And out of old books, in good faith,
Come all this new knowledge that men learn.

Geoffrey Chaucer, *Parliament of the Fowls*

There is only one thing for it then—to learn. Learn why the world wags and what wags it. That is the only thing which the mind can never exhaust, never alienate, never be tortured by, never fear or distrust, and never dream of regretting. Learning is the only thing for you. Look what a lot of things there are to learn.

T. H. White, *The Once and Future King*

PRE-RAMBLE

I want to begin this book with an anecdotal opening. This is an instance where a professor left me with several thoughts that contributed to how I communicate with the world around me.

I remember the first day in my survey of English literature class (the beginnings to the 1700s), when my professor, a medievalist versed in various languages and literatures, and a person who has forged an indelible mark in my education, stood in front of the board and asked us what the word "man" was in various languages, scribbling them down as we shouted answers in Spanish, German, Italian, Icelandic (as if any of us knew that), and Latin. When she was finished, we were left with an alternating list of words that seemed to look familiar in some places, but different in others:

English: man   Italian: *uomo*

Spanish: *hombre*   Icelandic: *mathr*

German: *mann*   Latin: *homo*

Now, if you look carefully, you'll see that the Romance languages (Spanish, Italian, and Latin) all look the same, while the Germanic languages (English, German, and Icelandic) all look the same. Over time, and geography, language mutates, migrates, and multiplies into other various forms and scripts, but everywhere you look, you can find threads connecting languages; you can discover historical and regional connections to languages and words all over the world, and if you tug at that thread, you discover that language is an ever-changing creature. I was in awe when I understood just how connected everything was by this weird concept called language.

Language is an ever-changing creature that adapts to the people of that time, and we, as people ever-striving, must constantly work to achieve the unachievable perfection in writing and in our grasp of language. And it's with our understanding of language and writing that we're able to convey our thoughts and ideas in a clear and precise manner. But not everybody has such a knowledge of writing: many breeze through high school and write their required papers, while never being taught the difference between "lie" and "lay" or how to properly integrate quotes, let alone how to even work with a text properly. These are the fresh new faces that show up in English 101 every year—the fresh new faces eager to learn. Eventually, it is through their hard work, silly mistakes, and learning from these mistakes that they come out better writers; they then apply these skills to all areas of their lives, whether it's drafting legal briefs for the boss, crafting poetry in some spare time, or filling out applications for graduate school. Writing is a skill one needs in everyday life.

And then there are the other students in my class, those who are not your traditional, fresh-from-high-school students. These are the students who I find, almost all the time, the most dedicated to education: they're returning to school after ten or so years and have never had a chance to attend college, so this is a new experience. Or they've maintained a job they got right out of high school, but no longer find it satisfying and wish to obtain a degree and an education that could lead to a more suitable career. One of my former students, for example, had been working for a cable company for many years, and in his forties decided he was sick of being yelled at by customers, so he decided to return to school for occupational therapy, something he viewed would be much more fulfilling. And oftentimes, despite their eagerness to learn, college proves to be very challenging: many older students never learned how to write a formal college essay, or they never had the need. But oftentimes it's these older students who work the hardest.

The idea for this book came from my experiences in classrooms that consisted of a jumble of students. The students I have taught and continue to teach, due to the nature of my college and the growing nature of colleges and universities around the nation, are students who vary in age and places in life. And because of this, writing takes a variety of forms for these students, but these varieties all center around the rhetoric of argument and persuasion. It's also because of this that we need to focus on multiple ways to teach writing. The specific idea of dissecting an essay arose from a conversation I had with one of these older students: he told me he understood everything I was teaching about the introduction, the conclusion, the use of body paragraphs to analyze and support the thesis, but he couldn't get the overall picture. This is what I want to teach my students: see the bigger picture. His struggle was seeing how everything fit together, how everything worked together in practice.

Because of this, I've decided to take a different approach. Previous writing books I've used or examined in passing are all strong in their own ways: they all give a good explanation of the various parts of an essay, they detail the uses and importance of tone and writing to the audience, there's special room for research and participating in the discourse; similarly, most of them come with some good reading comprehension and critical thinking practice, and exercises in thesis statements and tone—all at great length. I will always favor Strunk & White (*The Elements of Style*) for what it does as far as style and word choice. But what I really want to see is something that shows a sort of essay dissection, or an essay put into practice. In my class, I have students deconstruct articles in a way—we find the thesis, locate evidence and explanation, examine the transitions and flow of the essay as a whole, and attempt to understand how all of this comes together. Other textbooks I previously used were strong in their detailed and lengthy descriptions in theory, but I wanted to show my students, in practice, how an essay moves from general to specific, or unpacks textual support, or links together the conclusion.

This textbook will follow the construction of an essay (one I've written) on Mary Shelley's *Frankenstein*. My writing classes always follow some kind of theme, whether it's medieval romance or King Arthur in popular culture or the *Canterbury Tales* (I'm primarily a medievalist, after all), but one of my favorites to teach is the gothic novel. A monster in and of itself, the genre is a weird, shape-shifting thing that can be observed from multiple scopes of thought—feminist reading, or queer studies, or psychoanalysis, or whatever discourse we might be thinking in. My students have always taken a liking to my use of the gothic novel in my courses, so I thought this would be a good place to start.

In addition to all this, I got to thinking about Victor Frankenstein and his work as I brainstormed this book: he wanted to demonstrate his intellect and mastery over creation and human knowledge. In a similar way, students and academics alike (for even those high in the ivory tower are not inoculated against the pitfalls of writing) all try to grasp some mastery over writing; but the problem lies in the fact that writing, no matter how good you are, is something that takes continuous practice and work to get right. Wasn't it Hemingway who said, "We are all apprentices in a craft where no one ever becomes a master"? We, as writers, must work consistently to craft something that's worth reading; if we approach writing in an arrogant fashion, we're doomed to follow in Victor Frankenstein's path of failure (though most of us won't come close to creating a monstrous Creature).

Students and professionals alike all require practice in their crafts. I don't think I know one person who sets out to write without first having done some kind of prewriting or brainstorming. Our craft absorbs us and takes over our existence: consider how Frankenstein's months of work resembles that of the student locked away in the library for hours on end as he or she puts the finishing touches on their work—that had, of course, been written, rewritten, and revised many times:

The summer months passed while I was thus engaged, heart and soul, in one pursuit. It was a most beautiful season; never did the fields bestow a more plentiful harvest, or the vines yield a more luxuriant vintage: but my eyes were insensible to the charms of nature. And the same feelings which made me neglect the scenes around me caused me also to forget those friends who were so many miles absent, and whom I had not seen for so long a time. (34)[1]

And in a similar manner that Frankenstein crafted his Creature from different parts into one cohesive monstrosity, so do students craft essays from various parts that all work together to create one cohesive being—the various "bodies" that work together to support the introduction, or overarching claim.

I don't plan this book to be the only textbook in your class, nor do I want it to be. Good writing comes from reading good writing, and I believe the best way to learn to write is not to drill theoretical concepts into students' heads or have them do tedious reading exercises; I believe reading strong examples of writing and engaging with texts will result in good writing. And I don't believe a single textbook is best for reaching the optimum results, so using a writing textbook in unison to some critical text (e.g., *Frankenstein, Canterbury Tales, Jane Eyre, Dracula*, what have you) results in the best writing. Students must also rely on good teachers to leave quality feedback on their writing. To be frank, I took the very basics away from my own English 1010 (at my university we were on the four-digit system); my writing never developed or improved more analytically than when it was challenged in my upper-level English classes. This is where I would receive the most critical feedback on my ideas and my essay structure. I learned

---

1   All citations from *Frankenstein* appear within parentheses, and are taken from Mary Shelley, *Frankenstein*, ed. J. Paul Hunter, 2nd ed. (New York: W. W. Norton & Co, 2012).

best from written feedback and commentary. All in all, critical writing is built from critical thinking, and a stylebook on its own isn't sufficient.

We use the power of rhetoric and persuasion to stitch together our identities as professionals who are experienced and learned in many fields, from writers to academics, chemists to occupational therapists, lawyers to research analysts. Writing, and writing well for that matter, regardless of your age or career path, is essential in at once communicating effectively and clearly, and at the same time hollowing out a niche in the professional world.

CHAPTER I

Some Basics Before We Get Started

1. Summary vs. Analysis

One thing most students struggle with is the difference between summarizing a passage and analyzing a passage. There is a clear difference: summarizing is straight-to-the-point retelling the story you were writing about. This involves pointing the reader to interesting passages or plot points in the book, without expanding or pushing your ideas further: What does the passage say about the story overall? What do you think the author is trying to say? What does the red letter "A" symbolize?

These are all questions that English students are tired of hearing: "Not everything means something." Correct. But most of the time there is a purpose, or there is a message, or underlying statement: literature reflects the author's thoughts, either of themselves (internal, inward, introspective—those kinds of words), or of the world around them (the external, the contextual, the social-political). So instead of simply restating these plot points—annoying to the professor because they've already read the story and they don't want your glossing of it—you should consider what these plot points say or mean. My favorite question (which you'll see numerous times in this book) is, "So what?"

Mary Shelley didn't pick three books at random for the Creature to read, Bram Stoker didn't sic hyper-sexualized vampiresses on Jonathan Harker without intending to jab at sexually liberal women, and Chaucer didn't spend time fleshing out his character the Wife of Bath because he fancied her gap tooth. So the question here is if the scene, trope, theme, plot, event, character, or symbol means something, *what* does it mean? *How* does it mean this? And simply retelling the story will not answer this—you must do some deeper critical thinking. "If you're summarizing, you're not making an argument" is the old maxim English professors like to repeat again and again.

So how do we define summary? **Summary** is the act of condensing long works, chapters, novels, stories, or concepts down to their most basic and essential parts: the problem, however, is that it deals with a more surface-level reading of the text and doesn't address deeper thoughts in itself. You are restating, or highlighting, these essential components in your own words, but you're not asking the "So what?" Summarizing, however, is important: when you're introducing your audience (the reader of your paper) to an unfamiliar text, or a text they haven't read in a long time, some summary is necessary. It is necessary in supporting your deeper-level thinking and arguments, but it cannot stand on its own. Additionally, you need to relate whatever passages or plot points you're recalling to the overarching thesis of your paper. Don't throw in plot points that have nothing to do with your claim: if you're writing about the dangers of knowledge in *Frankenstein*, it's probably best to avoid summarizing Justine's trial.

The goal of the English 101 student is to push past this surface-level reading and deal with a deeper meaning—i.e., you need to do some sort of interpretive work and stake a claim from what you read. This is called analysis. **Analysis** is not pointing out obvious concepts in the text; it's picking out something new, or interesting, or confusing, or problematic; it's trying to understand and make sense of those things that are interesting, confusing, or problematic. This is where you explore the how and why a text says what it says (or means). This is also where you analyze areas of the novel in terms of relationships (how parts of the story work together); patterns, sequences, or design of the plot or themes; the role and purpose of certain characters or situations; the author's overarching point or meaning; and possibly the cause and effects that drive the plot. "So What?"

Here's the caveat: analysis should be in your own words. Don't just spit back what the professor has covered in class. A strong critical paper is one that demonstrates good analytical thinking of your own and in your own words. This is particularly important while writing a research paper (see Chapter III).

What follows is a brief list of literary terms that will come in handy while close reading and analyzing a work:

1. **Style** is the manner in which a particular author chooses to write his or her works. Style occurs in syntax (word order), structure, and organization of writing, and choice of diction.

2. **Diction** is the deliberate choice and use of words in writing or any form of communication. It's the choice of using "fall" instead of "autumn," or vice versa.

3. **Discourse.** Defined by Wikipedia:

"The totality of codified language (vocabulary) used in a given field of intellectual enquiry and of social practice, such as legal discourse, medical discourse, religious discourse, et cetera."

It is, in a general way, the discussion and intellectual enquiry of a certain topic in social structures. Think about feminism and racism; the way in which multiple discourses intersect is called

    intersectionality (e.g., discussing women of color in the discourse of feminism).

4.   **Antonym** is a word opposite in meaning of another.

5.   **Synonym** is a word with the same or similar meaning of another word.

6.   **Euphemism** is the replacement of words or phrases that are considered too harsh for words that are more polite; the phrase is an idiom, and does not retain its literal meaning. We tend to avoid directly saying "she died," so we use the more polite "she passed away."

7.   **Idiom** is a set of words that are not taken literally, but the phrase is understood to be something different than what the individual words mean: "He was sick as a dog."

8.   **Simile** is a figure of speech that draws a comparison between one thing and something completely different to establish a more vivid or emphatic description, often using the words "like" or "as": "He was brave as a lion."

9.   **Metaphor** is a figure of speech in which a word or phrase is applied to an object or action when it literally cannot be applied. Sometimes it's regarded as symbolic or representative of something.

All the world's a stage,
And all the men and women merely players
— Shakespeare, *As You Like It*

    The world is not literally a stage, but Shakespeare is trying to convey an understanding of how the world and its people work.

10. **Symbolism** is the use of symbols to represent ideas or qualities. Fire is representative of love, because of a burning passion. In the *Aeneid*, Dido is surrounded by various images of fire (her heart is aflame) to emphasize how much she is in love; likewise, she is symbolically consumed by love as she falls into a burning pyre.

11. **Foil** is a character who contrasts with the protagonist to highlight certain qualities in that character. In the *Harry Potter* series, Draco Malfoy is the foil to Harry Potter.

12. **Allusion** is a reference (usually indirect) that calls to mind something.

"Whiskey was his Achilles' heel" is a reference to the Greek hero Achilles in the *Iliad*, who was invincible, except for his heel. Whiskey was this man's weakness.

13. **Deus ex machina** means "god from a machine," and it describes when a seemingly unsolvable problem is suddenly and abruptly solved with the help of a contrived and unforeseen use or intervention of some other thing (character, object, event, ability).

In the Greek play *Medea*, the leading lady is presented, at the last second, with a dragon-pulled chariot to escape after committing some drastic murders.

14. **Foreshadowing** is when the author employs a hint to indicate something happening later in the story, in an attempt to avoid disappointment and arouse the reader. Sometimes characters will explicitly predict the future. And sometimes the author will drop hints to throw the reader off or mislead the reader—this is called a **red herring**.

Plot Structure

Additionally, while critically reading and referring to the points in a novel or story, it's rather important that you know the parts of the story. The basic structure of a story is as follows: exposition, conflict, climax, falling action, denouement (*Figure 1.1*).

Exposition is the introduction of the background information to the reader. For example, the setting, the characters and their backstory, and the events leading up to/before the main plot. In *Frankenstein*, the letters of Robert Walton and the story of Victor's childhood are the exposition. When we move from the setup to the actual problems in the story, we get conflict. **Conflict,** or the rising action, is the clash or incompatibility of two or more characters or forces (e.g., Man vs. Man, Man vs. Society, Man vs. Nature, or Man vs. Self). The conflict in *Frankenstein* is Victor's creation of the Creature and the subsequent abandonment of the Creature. This, with the actions of the Creature, complicates the plot and provides rising tension through the novel up until the climax.

Climax is the turning point in the action, or the highest point of excitement in the story. All the tension and suspense that had been building up in the conflict erupts with the Creature murdering Frankenstein's

PLOT STRUCTURE

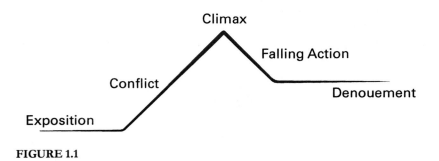

FIGURE 1.1

wife, Elizabeth. It's after this eruption in the plot that we get the falling action: **falling action** occurs typically near the end of the story when things start to die down and wrap up. For our novel, this is when Victor leaves to chase down the Creature.

Denouement is the final part of the narrative, also known as the resolution, in which the strands of the plot are drawn together and matters are resolved. This is like the conclusion of your paper. This is when Victor Frankenstein dies from exhaustion and illness, physically and mentally, from chasing after his horrendous Creature—who then wanders off into the cold on his own. The story is wrapped up, not happily ever after, and is brought to a close.

2. Close Reading

Close reading is not just skimming over the text and taking everything at surface value. It involves active engagement with the textual object. While reading, you should take the time to understand the basic concepts, themes, and problems of a text; you should always approach the text with the question, "What is this author trying to say?" As stated earlier, not everything means something, but much does, so it's always best to begin with this question in mind.

While reading, keep track of problems or themes or confusing instances in the passage. Underline **words** or **concepts** that are repeated through the text or carry significance, and highlight **themes** or important **dialogue**. Bookmark or dog-ear certain **passages** you want to return to, or write marginalia in your books. Keep an eye out for **patterns**, **contradictions**, and **parallelisms**. Keep asking questions of the text. If you are using a tablet or electronic version of a text, it's always useful to have a paper pad next to you ready for notes. I know my edition of *Frankenstein* is full of pen and pencil thoughts, and my copy of the *Morte Darthur* is half sticky notes (*Figure 1.2*).

The point here is to have your thoughts about the book or reading at hand: you want to be able to refer to areas of the text or to thoughts and ideas that the text is trying to make. It's not a good idea to rely on

FIGURE 1.2

memory to recall certain passages or ideas; not depending on memory makes it much easier to later find passages and quotes again for your paper. So always have a pencil or pen on hand while reading (unless for fun, nonacademic reading—but even then I like to annotate passages).

Summary and Analysis Addendum and Exercise

It's important to reiterate: the key difference between summary and analysis is looking deeper into the text. Don't simply retell what's going on in the story; push past your surface reading and see what the text is "doing," if a text can "do" anything at all. To grasp a deeper meaning of the text, break down the reading and evaluate the language the author is using, the way they present the work, the events, the actions, and the characters' dialogue and behavior.

Always consider:

- What does the author want us to think?
- What are the themes at work here?

- What is confusing or interesting to note?
- Where do you see patterns, why are there patterns, and where are the patterns different?
- What do the characters' actions and voice (dialogue, tone) reveal about their true selves, and how do these influence our liking or disliking of them?

Below are several passages. Your job is to evaluate each one and decide if the passage is more of a summation, or if there is a claim to be made there.

1. Malory's "Eve" comes to the reader in the form of Morgan Le Fey, foul enchantress and sister unto King Arthur. Unhappy with her role in life, Le Fey schemes against her noble brother to usurp his throne. She cares not if along the way she must cause the deaths of both her brother and husband, they are only men after all. Despite her cruelty and power she still requires the strength of men, not her own strength, to help her succeed. Morgan's plan can best be summarized by her lover and enforcer, Accolon.

2. *The Art of Courtly Love* by Andreas Cappellanus is based on different ways of loving. Andreas talks about the rejection of a lover and how love increases. He refers to jealousy as the nurse of love. In this reading you will read about more ways that make love increase in the medieval era.

3. The first book that he relates to the reader is *The Sorrows of Young Werter*, a very upsetting and emotionally torturous novel written by Goethe: "In the Sorrows of Werter, besides the interest of its simple and affecting story, so many opinions are canvassed, and so many lights thrown upon what had hitherto been to me obscure subjects" (89). Up until this point, the infantile Creature has learned of language, and he has learned Frankenstein's reaction to him, but he has not yet learned how to define and make sense of his Creator's reaction."

4. In Virgil's *Aeneid* Aeneas' journey is most influenced by the two main goddesses: Venus and Juno. Venus is the Goddess of Love, and she is Aeneas' mother. Venus would depict the "easy way" since she lets fate unravel and supports Aeneas on his journey. Meanwhile, Juno would be the "hard way." Juno is the husband of Jupiter and the Queen of the Gods. Juno plays the role of the main antagonist as she makes Aeneas' journey as difficult as possible.

5. The differences between Ligeia and Rowena are stunning, and they each stand for opposing positions of women in the world. Ligeia is from a suitably Gothic city—an ancient and decaying city—near the Rhine, and even more so, the narrator can reveal very little about her past, on account of the fact that he does not even know. She comes to the reader with neither parentage nor family name. All that we know of her is that she is Ligeia, and simply that—she is her own woman. Rowena, on the other hand, has a last name as well as an epithet: she is Rowena Trevanion of Tremaine.

3. The Types of Writing

At the most basic level, there are four types of writing:

1. Expository Writing

This is writing in which the author's purpose is to explain the subject matter or to inform the reader. Typically leaves out personal opinion and leaves us with facts and figures relevant to the material—look at the various "How-to" articles online, or look at a textbook.

2. Argumentative Writing

This writing states the author's opinion and attempts to influence or persuade the reader. Contains justifications and reasons to make someone believe the writer's point of view. Writer takes a stand on a topic, makes an argument with evidence and reason to back it up, and then asks you to believe their viewpoint. Will often call for an action from the reader.

3. Narrative Writing

This is when the author tells a story, which could be fiction or fact. Will typically include characters and dialogue, and there is a definite and logical beginning, interior, and an ending. Often there are actions, disputes, or problems and solutions.

4. Descriptive Writing

This is a type of expository writing that uses the five senses to paint a picture for the reader—uses imagery and specific detail. Spends time focusing on what can be heard, seen, tasted, felt, or smelled.

In professional and academic writing, you will most often be doing expository and argumentative writing, so it's important to have a good grasp of argument and critical reading (see Chapter II, Section 3: "The Thesis"). And even if you're not going to be writing thesis statements and academic papers your whole life, you'll need to understand the purpose and use of argument and persuasion—the cover letter, for example, is a form of persuasion where you give supporting evidence of your jobs skills and competence to a potential employer.

CHAPTER II

The Essay

1. Structure of the Essay

The basic structure of the essay is as follows. The essay, although a whole beast in itself, consists of parts and relies on these parts to work together in order to stand as a strong essay.

I. Introduction—an overview of the specific topic that narrows in scope toward a precise problem or topic of discussion
   A. THESIS—essentially what the paper is about.

II. Body—where you give your support and discuss your main points.
   A. First topic that supports your thesis.
   B. Second topic that supports your thesis.
   C. Third topic that supports your thesis.

III. Conclusion—wraps up all your main points and your argument; where you restate/paraphrase your thesis. But you do not copy and paste from the introduction.

All three parts—the introduction, body, and conclusion—work symbiotically, in an almost ring-like structure. The introduction lays the foreground of what's to be discussed in the essay while also explaining the significance of the problem or the argument in terms of the current scholarly discourse (e.g., "What current problems do Arthurian scholars have with the portrayal of Guinevere or Elaine of Corbyn?"). The body paragraphs detail the overall claim and also your reasons behind this claim, supporting it with textual evidence. And the conclusion wraps up everything you've just expanded, tying it all together in one nice, pretty package, and connecting it back to the introduction, coming full circle.

The circle and cohesive body are just a few ways of imagining the paper. One way that I was taught by a colleague was to view the paper as an architectural structure: the Temple of the Question, or the Temple that Worships the Question. For those who haven't seen this before, I've included a diagram of this layout (*Figure 2.1*).

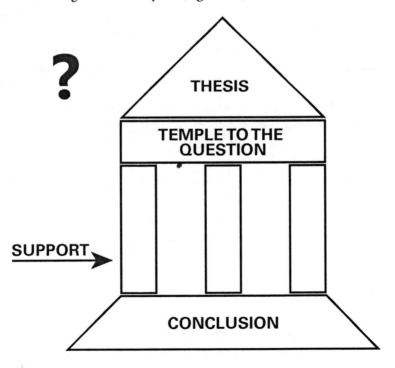

FIGURE 2.1

The Temple of the Question draws the metaphorical connection between the cohesive, coherent essay and the architectural structure of the temple. The foundation is the conclusion of the essay, upon which you support your thesis. The thesis statement—the claim, the most important part of the paper, the *whole purpose for* the paper—needs to be supported on a solid foundation. The columns are of course our support system, created from the textual evidence; you can't hold up your thesis or reach a conclusion without some sort of deductive reasoning and understanding of the text.

Below you will find more detailed explanations on how each paragraph should be set up, followed by a sort of essay "dissection" to **show** you how everything works in practice and not simply theory.

2. Prewriting

Every good writer has some method of prewriting; it's actually really hard to just jump right into the paper without first having mapped out a few things. Prewriting is a bit of an umbrella term that can include brainstorming, scribbling thoughts and ideas down on scrap paper, outlining, and really anything that gets thoughts onto paper where they can be organized.

I personally prefer some type of outline—the typical bulleted, Roman numeral outline. This is where I figure out my paper's main thesis and topic. What will I be writing about? What textual object will I be investigating? What will I be exploring or discussing or arguing? These are some basic questions to keep in mind when figuring out a topic for your English paper. Below you can find an example of the prewriting outline I drafted for the *Frankenstein* essay included in this book (*Figure 2.2*).

After determining the main topic of your essay, it's generally a good idea to craft a thesis statement, or at least a general thesis topic (the statement itself might be altered by the final draft). For my paper,

I want to explore Mary Shelley's ideas of appropriate knowledge, and I'll mostly be discussing Victor Frankenstein's Creature.

I then brainstorm areas of the Creature's knowledge and education that interest me the most, and it's the scene where the Creature finds the satchel of books that I think offers the most profound discussion on his education—at least according to Shelley. I pick three topics I want to discuss (or more, if you so please) and then give myself space to jot down ideas until I feel I've fleshed out enough to get started.

This outline is in no way absolute: topics might change—i.e., they could be added or subtracted as I'm writing, and some of the finer details might be left out entirely, but at that moment would have just needed to have been written down. That is, after all, the entire purpose of prewriting: you just need a space to throw everything onto paper, where you can pick things apart and organize, where you can pick and choose what is essential and what might in actuality be unnecessary for the paper. Just take all your thoughts down and cut as you go—this way everything doesn't end up jumbled together in your paper.

Now, of course, not everyone will be writing about *Frankenstein*. You might actually hate *Frankenstein*. But what I've laid out for you is a vague example of my writing process, where I start with some topic I'm interested in and make an outline. I consider what parts of the story are important in this topic, and I locate maybe one or several passages to discuss (depending on how in-depth I want to read or how important I find the passage to be in relation to my topic).

What you write about and how you write about it is all essentially up to you. But it's never a good idea to jump into battle without a plan of attack.

Frankenstein Paper

Dangers + uses of knowledge: Victor + Creature

Thesis - Shelley foregrounds an implicit stance on
acceptable knowledge and puts a limit on
the reach of human understanding.

* Proper education should consist of man's relation
to self, history, and religion

I. Werter - self
- understanding of emotions
- finds words to describe emotions
- connects with people through emotions - relatable, everyone
  has emotions

II. Plutarch - history
- high thoughts of morals
- the only men worth writing about in history are those
  of absolute virtue (heroes) or absolute vice (villains)
- archetypes of proper behavior - the Creature admires
  peaceable lawmakers and hates villainous behavior

III. Paradise Lost — religion
- most important: puts Creature in relation to Creator
  - he is to Victor as Adam is to God
- relates more to Satan however - desired love and
  protection but was denied both from Creator
  - rejected + ugly
- Frankenstein's papers were like the Creature's own
  form of Genesis (origin story)
- Creature recognizes Creator's power + the limit placed
  on those Created things
  - speaks to Victor's inability to see this limit
  - P.L: limit of knowledge to mankind by God (apple)
  - recognizes God's superior powers + asks for companion

FIGURE 2.1

3. The Thesis

Now, the most important part to your paper is your THESIS. Your thesis basically boils down to whatever your paper is about (topic, argument, the stance you take) into a succinct one- or two-sentence statement. It should be specific and clear, but not too specific. It should give me an idea of what your paper is about, what your argument is, and the stakes:

I argue X, because Y.

X is your stance on an argument. Y is your evidence and reasoning (do not LIST your evidence here, but give me a generalized reason that stands in for all your evidence). Until students get a grasp on implicit thesis statements, an explicit statement that follows this formula will suffice. Ask yourself "So what?" when thinking about your thesis: What are the stakes, what does this argument matter, and what does it tell us? What does it add to the current discourse on the subject? Connect to a larger issue.

Original thesis: *Frankenstein* is a novel about science and tragedy.

Okay, so what? Is this thesis specific, argumentative, and explanatory? No on all accounts. *Frankenstein* is, by definition, a novel and it is indeed about science and a tragedy of sorts. This is a vague statement, and it does not explain the purpose of the thesis: What exactly is this paper going to be about? Furthermore, it's not something that can be argued.

Revised theses: In *Frankenstein*, even though the Creature kills everyone close to Victor, there is still some humanity in him, illustrated by his remorse at the end.

Okay this is better. Now we understand what the paper is going to be about—the humanity of the Creature, despite all his evil actions. It is arguable, since your classmates might consider this remorse inadequate to make up for the Creature's killings. And, it's specific.

A final sidenote: It is really hard to PROVE something that is open to interpretation. Your argument shouldn't be to prove, but rather suggest or demonstrate something. That being said, avoid writing "prove" in your paper. Instead, use words such as "show," "demonstrate," "suggest," "illustrate," etc.

Argumentative Writing

The thesis statement is key to a strong argumentative paper—it provides guidance and focus, along with a substantial purpose for the paper. Without a strong thesis statement, your paper will tend to unravel or become unfocused. Things that a good argumentative paper should have are claim, substance, contestability, and clarity.

The claim is in your thesis statement and should offer some interpretation (or reading) of the text (or facts, if we're working within the realm of sciences—for now, we'll stick to humanities). The claim should flow logically with the remaining three aspects of argument; that is, the claim should also have substance, contestability, and clarity.

If something has **substance**, then it fulfills the "So what?" question. I often scribble "So what?" next to my students' thesis statements when there's little or no substance. It's pretty easy to just relay basic factual information from the text—e.g., "*Frankenstein* is about a man who creates life," "Victor and the Creature are both similar and different," or "The Creature is an evil person." What's more challenging, and what is more the mark of a good thesis statement, is taking these factual statements that are obvious, that make really no claim, and that are overly broad, and putting them up against the "So what?"/ "Why does this matter?" questions.

Writing a paper about the above three topics, without exploring why it matters, gives us nothing worth reading. Typically, these types of thesis statements preface papers that give more summary than insight. Let's have a look at these weak thesis statements and try to fix 'em:

1. "*Frankenstein* is about a man who creates life." Okay. This is obvious and pretty general. What does it matter if a man tries to create life? Something you could do is draw connections between Victor creating life and his tragedy of character. "Frankenstein argues that creating life is a trespass onto God's knowledge, and, therefore, that Victor was immoral in his actions."

2. "Victor and the Creature are both similar and different." As an English professor, one of the more common thesis statements that gets under my skin is the "both similar and different" claim. By and large, if you're talking about two things, they will obviously be different and similar. It's just a matter of fact. This is just fluff for the paper, where the student thinks he or she is making some kind of claim by pointing out that Thing One and Thing Two have differences and similarities.

   How do we fix this? Simple. Explain what the similarities and differences are, and why it matters to our understanding of the characters. A stronger claim would be: "While Victor was raised by loving parents and educated at the university, the Creature was quickly abandoned and left to teach himself the ways of life." But this does somewhat, admittedly, lack contestability.

   A good way of getting contrast across without explicitly having to spell out "similar and different" (last time I'm writing these words, I promise) is by using words that indicate this. Words such as "although" or "however" or "while," and using parallelisms, are all good means for a student to get contrasting attributes across to the reader.

3. "The Creature is an evil person." This is a weak thesis due to a number of qualities: it's loosely subjective (how do you define evil?), it's incredibly vague, and although it can be argued against, it lacks any substance (why does it matter if he's evil or not?). So how do we tackle this?

One place to start would be with defining evil, or in this case, explicating on what evil "things" the Creature does: the Creature kills William—Victor's brother—on accident and then kills several of Victor's other loved ones—the most unfortunate being Clerval. Murder is evil, even on accident. So therefore, the Creature's actions are evil. Now where's the substance? Why does this matter? A better way to approach this might be to examine the motives of the Creature.

To understand a character's actions in all literary studies, their motives—what drives them—is a good place to start. This is what makes characters most fascinating at times: for example, some of Shakespeare's most intricate and problematic villains are those whose motives are nigh impossible to discern. Both Iago (from *Othello*) and Aaron the Moor (*Titus Andronicus*) have provided innumerable English class essays due to their foggy motives.

So what are the Creature's motives? Where does he learn evil? From the pain he's felt from being rejected. So a better, more detailed thesis statement would be one that focuses on internal characteristics—on motives and morals and things similar. Instead of focusing on the overarching thematics of the novel, a student could potentially offer an in-depth character discussion. Better: "The Creature is justified in his evil actions because of the pain he has endured from society rejecting him."

All three of these statements are substantially stronger, and at the same time offer **contestability**, or the capability of being argued against. How do we know if your thesis has contestability? If one of your classmates can say, "No, you're wrong because of X, Y, and Z," then well done, you have contestability. Any thesis that evokes an argument, as opposed to "well, duh, that's obvious," is a strong thesis.

One classmate might go against "Frankenstein argues that creating life is a trespass onto God's knowledge, and, therefore, that Victor was immoral in his actions" and argue that creating life isn't immoral. Or perhaps one might say that the Creature is not justified in his murdering rampage. Your classmates would then need to provide evidence to support these counterarguments. It's in these arguments and counterarguments that academia finds discussion—and where discourse is defined when scholars interact back and forth between these points of contention, they are taking part in discourse. But we'll get to this later, when we enter the realm of the research paper.

Lastly, a strong thesis must have **clarity**. You need to be precise and concise in your writing, and try not to lose your reader. "Victor and the Creature are both similar and different" is not clear—I have absolutely no idea what your essay is going to be about. "While Victor was raised by loving parents and educated at the university, the Creature was quickly abandoned and left to teach himself the ways of life" is clearer, as now I know your essay is going to tackle the ideas of education. Perhaps a *contestable* thesis will argue that self-education is better than a university education?

More On Thesis Statements

A good way to help students think about thesis statements is to have them deal with a set of data from which two opposing or different conclusions can be drawn. As for literature, I like to give passages from a reading in class that have two completely different thematics. The student does not need to understand the reading or have knowledge of the reading outside of the passages; in fact, I like to give my students material they don't have context for. The objective rather is to have students work with this specific set of data (differing themes or tropes) and draw from only this to reach a conclusion. For example, below is an exercise that asks the students to write a thesis statement arguing whether *Sir Gawain and the Green Knight* is a religious poem or a medieval romance, based solely on the key passages provided.

Thesis Statement Exercise

The alliterative poem *Sir Gawain and the Green Knight* is supposedly written by an anonymous author called the "*Pearl* Poet," who also wrote a profoundly religious poem called *Pearl*. Read the two passages below, gather your evidence from the passages to substantiate your argument, and argue the following point with a clear and concise thesis statement: Is *SGGK* a religious poem, or a medieval romance (a tale dealing with chivalry, adventure, knights) based on these passages alone? It may be both, but your objective is to argue one over the other.

Excerpts from *Sir Gawain and the Green Knight* [1]

Part I

And when this Britain was founded by this rich knight
Bold men were bred therein, who loved fighting,
In many a difficult times troubles were wrought.
More marvels on this land have happened here oft
Than in any other I know, since that same time,
But of all that dwelt here of British kings,
Ever was King Arthur the noblest, as I've heard tell;
Therefore an adventure of the land I intend to show,
That a marvel in sight some men might consider it,
And a very strange adventure of Arthur's wonders.
If you will listen to this lay but a little while,
I shall tell it right away as I have heard in town
       with tongue.
   As it is put down and set
   In story firm and strong,
   With true letters fastened
   As this land has used longtime.
This king lay at Camelot upon Christmas;
With many worthy lords, men of the best,
Courteous of the Round Table all those rich brothers,
With rich well revel, and carefree mirth.
There jousted knights at times so many,
Jousted full merrily these noble knights.
Then they returned to court, to sing carols,
For their feast went on for fifteen days,
With all the food and the birth that men could devise,
Such noise and merrymaking, glorious to hear,
Pleasant noise all day, dancing at night.
All was happiness high in the halls and chambers,
These lords and ladies, the most pleasant to them it seemed.
With all the joy in the world they lived together,
The most famous knight under Christ himself,
And the loveliest ladies that ever have lived,
And he the handsomest king that ruled the court,
For all this fair folk in their first age
      in the hall.
   The happiest under heaven,
   King noblest man of mind;
   It was now very hard to reckon
   So hardy a host on hill.
       (lines 20-59)

Part 2

First, he was found faultless in his five senses,
And second failed never this knight in his five fingers,
And all his trust upon earth was in the five wounds
That Christ received on the cross, as the creed tells;
And wheresoever this man in battle was present,
His steadfast thought was in that, above all other things,
That all his fortitude he received from the five joys
That the high heaven queen* had in her child. *Mary
For this reason the knight fittingly had
In the inner half of his shield, her image painted,
That when he looked thereto, his courage never failed.
The fifth set of five that I find that the knight used
Were generosity, and fellowship above all things,
His purity and his courtesy crooked were never,
And pity, that surpasses all qualities, these pure five
Were more firmly fastened on that knight than on any other.
Now all these five groups, forsooth, were fixed on this knight,
And each one joined one another, and had no end,
And fixed upon five points, that failed never,
Nor came together on any side, nor came apart,
Without end at any corner anywhere, I find,
Wherever the pattern began or came to an end.
Therefore on his bright shield shaped was this knot,
Royally with red gold upon red gules,
That is the pure pentangle by the people called,
      in lore.
   Now prepared is Gawain fair
   And took his lance right there,
   And gave them all good day,
   He thought forevermore.

       (lines 640-669)

---

1 All citations from *Sir Gawain and the Green Knight* are of my own translation.

4. Tone and Style: The Introduction Paragraph

Start with a specific topic—e.g., treatment of Guinevere in medieval literature. Be sure to give the reader an interesting lead into the essay (the hook), but avoid "cosmic" over-generalizations (e.g., "From the beginning of time everyone has always said … ")

Bring the reader closer to the thesis, but don't jump right in. Give us details about the subject material to set up the introduciton: (1) give a little background info; (2) tell us why this is interesting; (3) tell us why it is important in the discourse of the material in general. Beware: avoid summarizing the story in whole; if you need to inform the reader or point the reader to specific events in the story, go ahead, but the introduction is not a summary of the story. More often than not I've read the book, so I already know what happens, but give enough detail to remind the reader of what plot points you'll be exploring.

The tone of your language and the style of your paper should be academic: this means avoiding slang or informal language; this means you aren't (re)telling a story, but exploring something that is troubling to the academic discourse. Tone also accounts for how you present your ideas: you want to set up your paper as an investigation of a topic through a textual/visual object. What is this book trying to say? What is this painting trying to say? For this to effectively take place in your paper, you must avoid writing in the first person: don't tell me what you think the book says (e.g., "I believe … "), rather simply tell me what the book says. First person pronouns ("I" or "me") and phrases such as "to me" should be left out of the paper: instead of saying "to me, Mary Shelley was arguing X," all you really need to say is "Mary Shelley argued X." This not only reads in a more professional and academic style, but it cuts out useless words.

Keep the paragraph moving. It should move from a general topic, to a more specific branch of that topic; e.g., how (specifically) Guinevere is portrayed. Give some key problems concerning the subject; i.e., how is Guinevere's portrayal different from the portrayal of other women in medieval literature, and what does this tell us?

After you've set us up with the important info for the background and introducing us to the topic, hit us with the THESIS.

- The thesis should be very specific to the subject matter and the text. The thesis should absolutely tell me what text or texts you're working with. I shouldn't have to guess.
- Tell me explicitly the stance you will take in your paper, and thereby the subject of the paper and argument. Tell me, in brief, the reasoning behind this stance. This will expand as the evidence in your body paragraphs.

I've addressed how to set up the introduction paragraph. Now, let's see it in practice. We'll take some time to do a close reading and dissection of the introduction to the *Frankenstein* essay "Mary Shelley's Educated Monster" (see Section 7: "The Whole Essay"). It might be a good idea to read the paper in its entirety before progressing.

Mary Shelley's *Frankenstein* is a Victorian-era morality play with the matter of knowledge at its crux: What knowledge is necessary in this world, how far should human knowledge reach, what qualifies as worthy knowledge? Grounded in the scientific revolution, Shelley launches a critique of the scientific expedition to ascertain the objective truth of the natural world—reflecting the fear and anxieties that accompany such an expedition. She centers on both Victor, the university-trained scientist who was raised in an idyllic childhood, and the Creature, an infantile being who was abandoned at an early age and must now educate himself, in order to explore these fears of expedition for the sake of knowledge. When Shelley has the Creature find a satchel of books (*Sorrows of Young Werther, Plutarch's Lives,* and *Paradise Lost*), he becomes enthralled by the contents of the writing, taking in everything he finds and using it to make sense of the world around him. Shelley uses this instance to both foreground an implicit stance on acceptable or necessary knowledge and to also contain the reach of human understanding. Shelley argues that a proper education consists of man's relation to the self, relation to history, and relation to religion.

A pretty lengthy introduction, but it works. Right from the get-go, we're introduced to the textual object that is the subject of the paper: **"Mary Shelley's Frankenstein is a Victorian-era morality play with the matter of knowledge at its crux."** The essay tells us it will be about Mary Shelley's *Frankenstein*, and also about the topic of knowledge.

The paper starts with the general topic of knowledge, and then it gets deeper: **"What knowledge is necessary in this world, how far should human knowledge reach, what qualifies as worthy knowledge?"** It's not just an essay about knowledge, but more specifically it examines the kinds, and with it the morals. This is greatly connected to the historical contexts, which the paper alludes to: **"Grounded in the scientific revolution, Shelley launches a critique of the scientific expedition to ascertain the objective truth of the natural world."** The background here is not overwhelming—the paper gives just enough information on the scientific revolution to set the mood. This then points us to the anxieties and fears associated with the gothic.

The writing then becomes even more focused, introducing us to the exact point in the novel that the essay will examine: **"When Shelley has the Creature find a satchel of books (*Sorrows of Young Werther, Plutarch's Lives, and Paradise Lost*)."** A specific passage is chosen that the writer believes is most important to explore in dealing with the general topic of knowledge. Lastly, the writer ends the introduction with a thesis statement:

Shelley uses this instance to both foreground an implicit stance on acceptable or necessary knowledge and contain the reach of human understanding. Shelley argues that a proper education consists of man's relation to the self, relation to history, and relation to religion.

One could argue that Shelley might not be saying anything on the limit of knowledge: I know I've had students argue with me that Shelley was more so speaking to the responsibility of having such knowledge. Either way, the thesis statement is **clear** in its formulation, prominently referring to the passage in the book and what this passage says, and it's **contestable** … but is it substantial? Does the author tell us "why it's important of the discourse of the material in general"? Not per se.

Since the paper only deals with a close reading of one object, it's not so much taking part in the discourse: it's not interacting with secondary sources, nor is it reacting to another academic's work. It does, however, implicitly answer the "So what?" question. The paper explores the ways in which Shelley comments against or critiques the scientific revolution: **"She centers on both Victor … and the Creature … in order to explore these fears of expedition for the sake of knowledge."** This paper is **substantial** in the ways it draws connections between this passage and Shelley's overarching message.

All in all, the introduction paragraph works. It flows from general to specific, it sets up some background to the text (both historical context and what passage is being examined), and it makes substantial and significant connections between this passage and why it matters in the overarching thematics.

Paragraph Formulas

Now that we've discussed introduction paragraphs, it's time to start building one. Here, and in other parts of the book concerning body and conclusion, I've provided a very primitive formula for structuring your paragraphs. These are not meant to build your work three sentences at a time, but rather think of these as the skeleton for larger ideas: your paragraphs need to have particular parts, and this will help you set it up. You must then choose where to expand your writing.

Introduction Paragraph Formula

Fill in these sections below; they are all essential to the introduction paragraph and fit with a clean formula. After you get the basics of the paragraph, then you can unpack and expand on your ideas. Remember, topic sentences should specify the text(s) you're working with and the thematic problems you'll be writing about.

Topic sentence/Hook

Context or unpacking of the topic

Thesis statement

Now that you have filled this out, what other material needs to be included? Where can you expand on your thoughts? This does not mean fluff up your introduction; this means you need to see where in your introduction you need to be more precise in your language and where you might need to explain something a bit beyond this formulaic set up.

Unraveling the Introduction

You have seen the textbook dissect the essay on *Frankenstein*, so now it's your turn to dissect an introduction. Read the following paragraph and answer the questions below while providing direct lines from the paragraph to substantiate responses.

From "Importance of *Linage* in *La Vie de Saint Alexis*," by Brendon Zatirka

> The 11th century *La Vie de Saint Alexis* is a peculiar vita in the fact that our saint, well, does not actively do much in the name of sainthood. He does not actively seek to convert others with the word of God, nor does he fight off demons like Saint Anthony or vanquish dragons like Saint George—mostly he just sits. He sits among the poor and then under the staircase of his estranged father's home, in an attempt to cut himself off from mundane possessions. In his impressive feats of asceticism, Alexis renounces and rejects everything that might impede him in his love for God—the world, his wife, and even his family, and eventually his will and subjectivity. In her chapter on our saint, Evelyn Birge Vitz explores the subjectivity of Alexis, as well as the subjectivity of everybody else in the vita. After examining Alexis himself and God as subjects, she calls into question the role of the family. She observes that the family is not merely an obstacle hindering Alexis' love of God, but something far more. However, she claims that the family doesn't act or behave as subjects. On the contrary, the family does in fact do a whole lot more: they act as subjects in consolidating Alexis' subjectivity. Despite the Saint's rejection of his family and lineage ("*parenz*" and "*linage*"), these relationships are invaluable subjects in and of themselves to Alexis' identity, and serve as catalysts to form his saintly renown.

1. What is the paper's main argument going to be? Provide the thesis statement.

2. What text is this paper going to be about?

3. What is the context of this paper?

4. What are some of the main themes and problems that the paper will address?

5. Logical Flow: The Body Paragraph

Body paragraphs are the bulk of your paper, and therefore, they are the part that carries the weight of your work. Each body paragraph focuses on ONE TOPIC; if you have too much going on, it might be time to insert a paragraph break. Think of each body as a mini-essay in and of itself. A good body paragraph consists of:

1. A topic sentence that flows smoothly and logically from the previous topic. It should begin in a general sense (that still relates to the topic at hand); we'll worry about specifics as we move into the paragraph. If you're trying to understand the character and motives of the Creature, it might be good to use one paragraph to talk about his reaction to society shunning and rejecting him. Good. Now we have a basic sense of what this paragraph will be about.

2. A claim: This is when you get more specific about the topic. You want to put forward some type of claim about the topic, something that can be reasonably deduced and that makes logical sense.
   a. For example, we want to claim that the Creature is justified in his murderous actions.
   b. You must be able to deduce a logical claim. Deductive reasoning means that a conclusion must be drawn from certain premises.

3. Evidence: Academic papers require evidence, meaning you must back up your logical claim with textual support. No ifs, ands, or buts in my class. You will be pulling quotes from the text, and introducing them with a COLON, as such: "I am malicious because I am miserable; am I not shunned and hated by all of mankind?" (102).

4. An explanation of this evidence. You can't just throw a quote into a paper without an explanation, and you may not in any way conclude the paragraph with a quote: you MUST explain. And by explaining, I mean you must:
   a. Unpack the quote by giving your own understanding of the quote. What precisely is the author saying? So, quite literally, the Creature claims he is only evil because of his rejection from society and the ways people have treated him.
   b. Explain the quote's relevance to the claim, and to the overarching argument of the paper.

5. Concluding statement. This pretty much goes together with explaining the evidence to your claim. You need to take this last space to

connect this particular topic (i.e., the Creature's morality and immorality) to the thesis statement.

And always remember:
EVERYTHING MUST TIE BACK TO THE THESIS STATEMENT.

Following this will assure a well-written body paragraph.

One thing you might want to do is not only take this space to support your own claim, but also offer a rebuttal. You might claim the Creature is, in fact, justified, whereas somebody else can just as easily argue he was not.

You will want to present this counterargument and knock it down. Poke holes in claims and offer counterevidence against them (that supports your take on the material). This makes your claim seem stronger. If you're able to defend your claim against a counterargument, you will have a higher chance of winning the reader over and having him or her align with your side.

Incorporating Quotes Into Your Paper

Incorporating quotes into your paper is essential when supporting your claim. When arguing something about a text, you need to demonstrate a basic grasp of deductive reasoning, and you need to demonstrate that you actually understand what the author is saying. Shame on the student who supports a claim with irrelevant or misunderstood quotes. You want to think about integrating quotes in a sandwich form:

State your claim:
    "Give your evidence" (Malory, pp. 128–129).
And then unpack and explain.

Things to remember: you introduce a quote with a COLON (:). Until you grasp this essential aspect, do not try to integrate any other way. And also remember that you NEVER end or begin a paragraph with a quote. You also do not begin a sentence with a quote: it should be incorporated into a sentence that's already going.

You must attribute the quote (name the author) and cite the location in the text, either by page number or line number—ex: According to Thomas Malory, ladies of the medieval court were only ever damsels in distress: "And then give me a quote from the *Morte Darthur* that backs this up" (pp. 128–129). And then you would unpack the quote and tell me its relevance to the claim. Note: if you mention the author's name up front, you do not need to include it within the parentheses.

Again, we'll explore how the body paragraph works in practice by breaking down an example from our essay (see Section 7).

> It is also worth noting that as the Creature finds himself in Adam, he understands the subordination of mankind to God, and if any tale is the quintessential parable against trespassing on God's knowledge, it's that of Adam and Eve's expulsion from Eden.

This is drawn from the last body paragraph (before the conclusion), and as you can see, it sets up exactly what this paragraph is going to be discussing. The topic is that of religion and the Creature finding a connection to Adam. **"It is also worth noting"** draws a nice connection with the previous paragraph, which focused on the Creature's interactions with John Milton's *Paradise Lost*.

While you don't have to use explicit transition words, you do need to show some act of transition and connection. Jumping around topics is hard on the reader, so your topics should be related and "stitched together" in cohesion.

After we're led into this topic with a logical flow, the essay hits us with a mini-claim, i.e., the claim of this paragraph: **"For Mary Shelley to include** Paradise Lost **in the Creature's upbringing is to imply that part of a necessary education is knowing there is a limit to human understanding."** The writer draws a logical conclusion from this passage and the Creature's reading of *Paradise Lost*; if he read the book and saw himself as Adam, then the Creature would have deduced that some knowledge is good and some is bad, **"that there is some natural limit over which man should not reach."** And after stating this claim, the writer gives us some textual support.

The textual support is not from *Frankenstein*, but from *Paradise Lost*. Here the writer is doing some intertextual work, drawing connection between the actual story in *Frankenstein* and how it interacts with *Paradise Lost*. Regardless, the paper supports its claim: **"such commission from above/ I have received, to answer thy desire/ Of knowledge within bounds"** and cites it (VII. 118–120). This way, we know that the writer is sure of the meaning of the text. This is where unpacking and explaining the text becomes important.

Directly after this textual support the writer explains: **"Raphael prefaces his answer with a warning against exploring beyond the boundaries that God has placed on our understanding."** This gives us an understanding of what the writer draws from the text and can deductively conclude based on their interpretation. The remainder of the body paragraph makes the connection back to *Frankenstein* and the main claim of not only this particular body paragraph, but also of the entire essay.

And if this is the Creature's moral of the story—that mankind should stick to its realm of knowledge—then it underscores Victor's lack of proper education. Through religion, the Creature learns of the dangers of seeking God's knowledge, whereas Victor lacks this insight.

We can see how the author relates Raphael's warning to the Creature's own education of the rights and wrongs of knowledge. And after that the writer then connects all of **this back to the thesis** concerning the importance of religion in the Creature's education and the limit on knowledge.

Think of each body paragraph as a mini-essay, in which you have the topic, the claim, the support, the exposition, and the conclusion. In fact, each body paragraph should work together with the rest of paper, related and connected in tone and importance to the whole cohesive body.

Body Paragraph Formula

Fill in these sections below; they are all essential to the body paragraph and fit with a clean formula. After you get the basics of the paragraph, then you can unpack and expand on your ideas. Remember, topic sentences should specify ONE of the subjects and topics covered in this paper; do not try to fit more than one topic in one paragraph.

Topic sentence

Main problem and your claim

Textual evidence to support the above claim

What does the quote actually say?

<u>What is the significance of the quote in relation to the thesis?</u>

<u>Wrapping up</u>

Now that you have filled this out, what other material needs to be included? Where can you expand on your thoughts? This does not mean fluff up your paragraph; this means you need to see where in your writing you need to be more precise and where you might need to explain something a bit beyond this formulaic set up. Is everything related? Do you have material that is irrelevant and needs to be cut?

Unraveling the Body

You have seen the textbook dissect the essay on *Frankenstein*, so now it's your turn to dissect a body paragraph. Read the following passage and answer the questions below while providing direct lines from the paragraph to substantiate responses.

From "Importance of *Linage* in *La Vie de Saint Alexis*," by Brendon Zatirka[1]

> The people, urgent to save themselves and Rome, run to Eufemian, to the head of Alexis' noble lineage, and inquire the whereabouts of "the one who sits." It is not until after Alexis passes away that his subjectivity is confirmed: first, that he is in fact the man of God (343), and then again when his letter is read. The letter connects Alexis to the lineage from which he estranged himself, and which will now serve as an invaluable indicator to who he is: "the letter told them of his father and of his mother, and it also told

---

[1] All translations for *La Vie de Saint Alexis* are my own.

them from which lineage he was" (379–80). The revelation of his lineage is thereby a revelation of his subjectivity, and thus the people are finally able to name him and venerate him. It is important to call attention to the actual naming of Alexis: it is neither the Pope, nor the cleric, nor anybody from the crowd who acknowledges his christening, but rather his lineage. In the session of grieving, the family goes in order, from father to mother and then wife, to lament the loss of Alexis, and also confirm his subjectivity by confirming his name. Eufemian cries, rather loudly, so that everyone around may hear. Grief-stricken, he claims "O son Alexis, what dolor comes to me!" both indicating his name, and his noble lineage—the fact that he is Eufemian's son. In fact, both the father and mother repetitiously vocalize both his name and his status as son through their cries. They amplify through repetition the sorrow that comes from this honorable man's death and the pain felt by the family; they also elucidate his subjectivity and connection to this lineage. The wife, now a member of the family, laments and indicates him to be her husband and lord, calling him "Sire Alexis" and "*kiers amis*" [dear friend]—a term of affection. She also positions herself next to Alexis as a former wife by claiming "Now I am a widow" (491). The whole family collaborates to position Alexis back into his subjectivity; we, and the people, now know that he was a son and a husband belonging to a *halt parentét*, which is invaluable to his veneration.

1. What is the main topic or problem that this paragraph is trying to unpack?

2. What is the overarching claim of this paragraph?

3. Evaluate how well the author unpacks their textual support. Remember, this means literally explaining the quotation for the reader and also explaining its significance to the overarching topic.

4. What is the main takeaway of this paragraph?

6. Dropping the Mic: The Conclusion Paragraph

The conclusion is the final part of your essay. That being said, there should be no new information brought up here.

The conclusion relies on circular composition; your essay should flow like a ring. Using only the material you have already presented in this essay, you should wrap up everything in a nice little package. By stuffing new information that wasn't introduced earlier, you make this package a little untidy and overflowing.

You should:

1. Restate the topic and thesis of the essay. Do not copy and paste the thesis, but rather paraphrase it.

2. Revisit your main points and draw connections between them and your thesis. Remember, everything must connect.

3. Emphasize the importance and significance of the essay; i.e., what does all of this say about the treatment of women in classical literature?

Remember, it's really hard to PROVE something that is open to inter-pretation. Your argument shouldn't be to prove, but rather suggest or demonstrate something. As such, avoid using "prove" in your paper.

Your paper can end itself by calling the readers to action. Perhaps they're not satisfied with your reading, so they will then do their own reading and quite possibly argue against your claims. This is where most academic writing comes from—one person will write an article and make a claim about something, and a reader who disagrees will then write their own article refuting the first author. Academia, after all, is simply a world of discussion and discourse. Or perhaps the paper will draw the reader to a really interesting point, and then the reader will want to see if this same interpretation and conclusion can be drawn in other bodies of literature (e.g., can the same problems of gender in Chaucer's *Canterbury Tales* also be explored in Malory's *Morte Darthur*?).

Don't be vague or wishy-washy. Be assertive in your paper, up until the very end. There's a phrase in popular culture called "dropping the mic," a figurative action that occurs when you best somebody or win an argument with overwhelming conviction. There is no chance for a comeback, there is no chance for a response. It's over. Think of your conclusion as such: if you can't imagine yourself dropping the mic after the final sentence in your essay, your conclusion needs to be stronger. You want the reader to be blown away with how you've presented your evidence and how you've supported your claims. You want to end your essay—which you've spent hours, days even, writing—with overwhelming conviction.

What follows is our conclusion in practice, just like our preceding chapters on the introduction and body. Here is the conclusion para-graph from our essay (again, refer to Section 7 of this chapter for the entire essay).

In sum, Mary Shelley encircles human understanding with lofty hedges built from the only knowledge necessary in mankind's education: (1) the self's perception of its internal reflections and emotions; (2) history's virtuous heroes and abhorrent villains, whose morals mankind should follow and whose vices mankind should reject; and (3) the relation to God's superiority, coupled with the parable concerning the dangers of God's knowledge. Shelley grapples with the fear and anxiety during the scientific revolution and addresses the dangers that come with such an exploration of the world around them. To exemplify this, she has Victor Frankenstein climb over the hedges of Eden, where he trespasses on God's knowledge, only to be struck down by tragedy when he can't handle the responsibility of his Creature. To Shelley, there are some things that should just never be known.

Again, we need some kind of transition—a sign or indication that the end is near. Sometimes, after reading a long and intensive paper, that final transition is like an oasis in a desert. My favorite ways to draw things to a close include "in sum," "in conclusion" (tired, tried, and true), "finally," or "in the end." There are literally dozens of ways to indicate the paper has transitioned from evidence, support, and analysis to wrapping up and drawing conclusions.

Just like every other paragraph in the paper, you should lead into the conclusion with a topic sentence, preferably one that encapsulates the message of the entire paper. This is where you could allude back to the thesis (since everything connects back to the thesis), but without copy and pasting it: **"Mary Shelley encircles human understanding with lofty hedges built from the only knowledge necessary in mankind's education."** Recall the original thesis statement: "Shelley uses this instance to both foreground an implicit stance on acceptable or necessary knowledge and contain the reach of human understanding."

Our topic sentence reminds us of Shelley's critique on the reach of human knowledge, as well as her intent to offer a limit to it. Next, we want to tie together all our main points, which this conclusion does:

1. The self's perception of its internal reflections and emotions.

2. History's virtuous heroes and abhorrent villains, whose morals mankind should follow and whose vices mankind should reject.

3. The relation to God's superiority, coupled with the parable concerning the dangers of God's knowledge.

This reminds us of all the major elements this paper has addressed: it at once keeps it short and simple, and at the same time draws them together into one coherent conclusion. All points of your paper should relate to one another, and everything should connect cohesively.

The remainder of the conclusion should be left for explicating very little. Draw some type of conclusion (via deductive reasoning) from your analysis, explain how the main points fit together in this conclusion, and end on some final words. You want your reader to walk away from your paper convinced of your analysis and of your ideas. This means this is not the time to add new details that were not brought up in the paper earlier. Likewise, this is not the place to suggest what the characters "should" have done, or what they "could" have done. It's not your job to supply alternative endings or suggest hypothetical situations. Shoulda-coulda-woulda conclusions are weak and thereby weaken your overall message. Keep it to the facts—the concrete details in the story and what actually happens in the story. This is what your analysis and conclusion should focus on.

Lastly, you want to end on a strong note. Something witty or biting, or some final and quick statement that sums up everything would be a nice way to end your paper: **"To Shelley, there are some things that should just never be known."** It's short, sweet, and to the point, and it embodies the fears and anxieties that this paper set out to explore.

Conclusion Formula

Fill in these sections below; they are all essential to the conclusion and fit with a clean formula. After you get the basics of the paragraph, then you can unpack and expand on your ideas. <u>Remember, this is not a place for new material.</u>

<u>Transition into the conclusion</u>

<u>Rephrasing of the thesis statement</u>

<u>What were the main points of your paper?</u>

<u>What conclusion can we reach from this evidence?</u>

<u>Final statement</u>

Now that you have filled this out, what other material needs to be included? Where can you expand on your thoughts? This does not mean fluff up your paragraph; this means you need to see where in your writing you need to be more precise and where you might need to explain something a bit beyond this formulaic set up. Is everything related? Do you have material that is irrelevant and needs to be cut?

Unraveling the Conclusion

Just a reiteration of the exercises before: you have seen the textbook dissect the essay on *Frankenstein*, so now it's your turn to dissect a conclusion. Read the following paragraph and answer the questions below while providing direct lines from the paragraph to substantiate responses.

From "Importance of *Linage* in *La Vie de Saint Alexis*," by Brendon Zatirka

> In sum, although this vita might be *La Vie de Saint Alexis*, it is not enough to write off the family of Alexis as merely obstacles to his sainthood. The focus might be on Alexis, but the majority of the text concentrates on the reaction of those surrounding the saint, i.e., his family and the people of Rome. A generous amount of space is given to the lamentations, prayers, and commemorations of everyone who is not named Alexis, it would, therefore, be obviously imperative to elucidate their roles throughout the narrative. The family is not just a highlight of ordinary mortals gone wrong, but rather they are the movers of the plot, first as the high and wealthy nobility that Alexis must give up, and then again as the force that confirms the dead saint's name. Throughout the poem, Alexis denies every aspect of his subjectivity, rejecting his lineage and inheritance, and then starts rejecting his will and his corporeality until he is finally no more, all so that he may serve and love God. It is through this lineage that the people of Rome hear the saint's name, and that his subjectivity is consolidated and brought back into existence; thus he becomes a subject to whom they may pray—but only, of course, after he fully reaches his goal of being a most holy man.

1. Remind us again what the thesis of this paper is: provide a sentence or two from this paragraph only.

2. What were some of the main points to the paper?

3. What would you say is the conclusion of this argument?

4. Is there anything else that we can take away?

7. Last Touches on Your Paper

Below you will find information on paper titles, along with a final checklist to run through as you finish putting the last touches on your paper.

Catchy Paper Titles

In actual professional practice, academics always include some kind of title to their paper. These tend to stray from basic titles like "Bram Stoker's *Dracula*." The title is the very first thing your audience will read: you'll want to think of this as part one of your hook (the other part being your actual hook in the introduction), so a good title is necessary. Its main function is to reveal the topic of the paper, catch the reader's interest, and reflect the tone of the piece.

You should include key terms in your title: these key terms should point out the topic, thematics, concerns, or subject material of the paper. You must also indicate the textual object (naming precisely what text/book you're writing about). Having witty titles helps. But having informative titles is more important.

Here are some examples:

- Source, Authority, and Audience in BBC's *Merlin*, by Jon Sherman
- Symptomatic Subjects: Bodies, Signs, and Narratives in Late Medieval England, by Julie Orlemanski
- Sui Generis: The Architectonics of the Alliterative Morte Arthure, by Elizabeth S. Sklar
- Sex, Power, Business: Chaucer's Subversive "Wife of Bath," by Brendon Zatirka

You must include a title on your papers. One popular way of making a title is starting with a quote or witty phrase followed by a colon, and then a more detailed explanation. (That's what all the academics do!) In order to gain a better understanding of how titles should look and function, peruse any number of academic articles and see how the authors have formatted their titles: consider whether there is lacking information, whether it hooks your interest, or whether you have any idea what they're writing about at all.

Critical Paper Checklist

Here is a fancy checklist of all sorts of things that might show up in a final paper for an English composition class. Go through the checklist and make sure you're not doing all the wrong things, and make sure you're doing all the right things.

- ☐ Do you have a strong thesis? Where is it? Is it at the end of the introduction?

- ☐ Do you use the pronoun "I" or "me" in your paper anywhere (other than textual support)? If so, delete it all.
- ☐ This is not a paper of what you "believe" or "think," nor is it about your "opinion." These words should not show up in your paper; this is an exercise in exploring what the TEXT says. Simply state your claim (without prefacing with "I believe that") and back it up.
- ☐ Are you giving me a critical reading, or are you summarizing the story for me? Do not summarize—remember this.
- ☐ Are you being too vague in your writing? You don't want to be overly general, particularly in your introduction: you must be precise and specific, otherwise I'll believe you did not actually do your readings.
- ☐ Make claims based on the specific reading; do not make generic claims or claims based on general contextual background information.
- ☐ Check your spelling. Check your capital and lowercase letters.
- ☐ Are your paragraphs indented?
- ☐ Do you use the words "seems," "might," "maybe," "something," "someone," or anything in this same category of vague language? Delete it and be specific.
- ☐ Do you say "this quote means"/"this passage means"? Don't do it.
- ☐ Is all your punctuation correct? Remember, you introduce quotations with colons.
- ☐ AVOID should, could, would situations. You're job is not to come up with hypotheticals or to write alternative endings to our books; your job is to deal with what ACTUALLY happened in the story and interpret/critically analyze that.
- ☐ Are you using textual support? You need to reference specific scenes or incidents to substantiate your argument.
- ☐ Remember GOOGLE is your friend for any formatting problems you might have.

☐ The Reader! Keep the reader in mind—that is to say, don't assume the reader knows everything you're talking about, but at the same time, there's no reason to summarize the entire story (just so you can take up valuable essay space). Give the reader important and vital information so that they understand your paper; sometimes when you make a point, you need to explain what you mean. Don't feed them irrelevant summary and plot points.

☐ TITLES. Big works (novels, TV series, films, plays, albums) are all underlined OR italicized. Smaller works (short stories, poems, articles, TV episodes, songs) are all put in "quotation marks."

☐ No logograms or punctuations to replace words. Do not use slashes: you can find other ways to write what you're trying to write. Additionally, replace each & (ampersand) you write with the word "and."

☐ Don't bother saying "in the novel/story, this event happened." We know that it's in the story. Just tell us what the event is.

8. The Whole Essay

Below is an example essay written to accommodate most English 101 courses: it is an in-depth analytical reading of a singular text—albeit there is some handling of supplementary sources—and this reading concerns one particular theme or passage in the text.

When I teach *Frankenstein*, my discussion has much to do with the treatment of knowledge and the anxieties that come with it; therefore, the essay that follows focuses on the Creature's education and his interaction with the three books he finds: *Sorrows of Young Werter*, *Plutarch's Lives*, and *Paradise Lost*. There is some minor interaction with *Paradise Lost*, only to supplement the close reading of this scene, but as a whole, the essay is focused in a manner that students of English 101 should be able to emulate (as opposed to hopping all around).

Mary Shelley's Educated Monster
by Brendon Zatirka

But knowledge is as food, and needs no less
Her temperance over appetite, to know
In measure what the mind may well contain
Oppresses else with surfeit and soon turns
Wisdom to folly as nourishment to wind.
— John Milton, *Paradise Lost* (VII. 126–30)[1]

Mary Shelley's *Frankenstein* is a Victorian-era morality play with the matter of knowledge at its crux: What knowledge is necessary in this world, how far should human knowledge reach, what qualifies as worthy knowledge? Grounded in the scientific revolution, Shelley launches a critique of the scientific expedition to ascertain the objective truth of the natural world—reflecting the fear and anxieties that accompany such an expedition. She centers on both Victor, the university-trained scientist who was raised in an idyllic childhood, and the Creature, an infantile being who was abandoned at an early age and must now educate himself, in order to explore these fears of expedition for the sake of knowledge. When Shelley has the Creature find a satchel of books (*The Sorrows of Young Werther*, *Plutarch's Lives*, and *Paradise Lost*), he becomes enthralled by the contents of the writing, taking in everything he finds and using it to make sense of the world around him. Shelley uses this instance to both foreground an implicit stance on acceptable or necessary knowledge and contain the reach of human understanding. Shelley argues that a proper education consists of man's relation to the self, relation to history, and relation to religion.

Having learned language from the De Lacy family, the Creature is set with a foundation for interacting with the world: he now has the basic knowledge of the symbolic world and is able to explore the conduits by which knowledge is transferred—in reading and in speaking, such as when he hears Felix instructing from the *Ruins of Empires*. The Creature finds a satchel in the back of the cottage that contains three books: "I can hardly describe to you the effect of these books. They produced in me an infinity of new images and feelings" (89).[2] It is in these books that the Creature takes his first plunge into the world of sentimentality and emotions.

The first book that he relates to the reader is *The Sorrows of Young Werther*, a very upsetting and emotionally torturous novel written by Goethe: "In *The Sorrows of Young Werther*, besides the interest of its simple and affecting story, so many opinions are canvassed, and so many lights thrown upon what had hitherto been to me obscure subjects" (89). Up until this point, the infantile Creature has learned of language, and he has learned Frankenstein's reaction to him, but he has not yet learned how to define and make sense of his Creator's reaction. In Goethe's novel, the Creature learns of an individual who has been rejected by the one he loves, which produces a multitude of feelings in the Creature: first, he learns the words to describe this feeling—that of abandonment—and second, he learns empathy, the ability to connect with what others feel. Through this, the Creature discovers relationships between individuals and defines the existence of an individual (the self).

He feels what Werther feels: "I inclined towards the opinions of the hero, whose extinction I wept, without precisely understanding it" (89). At first, he does not know why he's weeping, but he learns it's because he found himself in the situation, in this feeling of rejection and abandonment. This drives the Creature to question his sense of self, of which he knew nothing: "Who was I? What was I? Whence did I come? What was my destination?" (89). Shelley mounts an argument that the first and foremost knowledge in education (after language, of course) is man in relation to the self; this curiosity to figure out more of himself—who he is—urges the Creature onward.

The second book that the Creature recounts is a volume of *Plutarch's Lives*. Those familiar with the classical world know that Plutarch was a Greek historian who recorded the lives of ancient rulers and worthy individuals, such as Julius Caesar, Mark Antony, and Alexander the Great. The Creature claims *Plutarch's Lives* taught him "high thoughts" and "to admire and love the heroes of past ages" (89). While Werther taught the Creature how to understand his emotions, the history of classical heroes teaches him about admirable virtues and morals that Frankenstein failed to impart as a father figure. He exclaims:

> I read of men concerned in public affairs governing or massacring their species. I felt the greatest ardor for virtue rise within me, and abhorrence for vice, as far as I understood the signification of those terms, relative as they were, as I applied them, to pleasure and pain alone [. . .] I was of course led to admire peaceable law-givers. (90)

Who are the people worth writing about in history? Those of absolute virtue or of absolute vice—according to Plutarch, at any rate. The Creature learns to admire those who have virtuous morals and engender pleasure—such as the "peaceable law-givers"—and to reject those who are villainous and cause pain. Since the Creature perceives the world through the perception of pain and pleasure, he comes to associate morals with pleasure as desired behavior; he wishes not to inflict pain similar to that which he has felt. It is through history and those worth being remembered that the Creature learns of right and wrong.

Lastly, the Creature recounts his interaction with John Milton's *Paradise Lost*. It is this text—one rooted in religion—that the Creature treasures and relates to most. It is also this text that speaks most to Victor Frankenstein's reach for knowledge and underscores the limits of human understanding. The Creature exclaims that, like Adam, he "was created apparently united by no link to any other being in existence," but unlike Adam—who "was allowed to converse with, and acquire knowledge from beings of a superior nature"—he "was wretched, helpless, and alone" (90). Even though the Creature recognizes that he is similar to Adam in their creations and their relation to a creator (he is to Victor as Adam is to God), he is not accepted or treated with the benevolence that God had treated Adam. Rather, the Creature makes a deeper connection with Satan, "the fitter emblem to [his] condition" (90). On the other hand, the Creature complains that, like Satan, he was rejected and expelled from God's love: "for often, like him, when I viewed the bliss of my protectors, the bitter gall of envy rose within me" (90). The happiness and love that the De Lacy family shared for one another and that his creator denied him, made the Creature jealous. Through religion, the Creature found that the Creator is supposed to be a source of love and protection, neither of which he received from Victor.

It is also worth noting that as the Creature finds himself in Adam, he understands the subordination of mankind to God, and if any tale is the quintessential parable against trespassing on God's knowledge, it's that of Adam and Eve's expulsion from Eden. For Mary Shelley to include *Paradise Lost* in the Creature's upbringing is to imply that part of a necessary education is knowing there is a limit to human understanding. The Creature would have learned from Adam and Raphael's interaction that knowledge can be good and bad, and that there is some natural limit over which man should not reach. Adam, driven by the same curiosity as Victor, asks Raphael the creation story, and Raphael responds:

> such commission from above
> I have received, to answer thy desire
> Of knowledge within bounds; beyond, abstain
> To ask; nor let thine own inventions hope
> Things not revealed, which the invisible King,
> Only Omniscient, hath suppressed in night. (VII. 118–123)

Raphael prefaces his answer with a warning against exploring beyond the boundaries that God has placed on our understanding; he allows Raphael to recount the creation story to Adam, but beyond that, Adam ought not seek. With this warning, mankind should not ponder those "things not revealed," which God "hath suppressed." And if this is the Creature's moral of the story—that mankind should stick to its realm of knowledge—then it underscores Victor's lack of proper education. Through religion, the Creature learns of the dangers of seeking God's knowledge, whereas Victor lacks this insight; his hubris knows no boundaries and it is this intrusion by creating life that leads to Victor's tragedy of character.

In sum, Mary Shelley encircles human understanding with lofty hedges built from the only knowledge necessary in mankind's education: (1) the self's perception of its internal reflections and emotions; (2) history's virtuous heroes and abhorrent villains, whose morals mankind should follow and whose vices mankind should reject; and (3) the relation to God's superiority, coupled with the parable concerning the dangers of God's knowledge. Shelley grapples with the fear and anxiety during the scientific revolution and addresses the dangers that come with such an exploration of the world around them. To exemplify this, she has Victor Frankenstein climb over the hedges of Eden, where he trespasses on God's knowledge, only to be struck down by tragedy when he can't handle the responsibility of his Creature. To Shelley, there are some things that should just never be known.

Notes

1. All citations from *Paradise Lost* appear within parenthesis, and are taken from John Milton, *Paradise Lost*, <http://www.paradiselost.org/8-Search-All.html>.
2. All citations from *Frankenstein* appear within parentheses, and are taken from Mary Shelley, *Frankenstein*, ed. J. Paul Hunter, 2nd ed. (New York: W. W. Norton & Co, 2012).

CHAPTER III

The Research Essay

1. Research: Finding a Topic

The research aspect of a paper is usually a step up from your typical close-reading essay. For a research paper, when writing, you'll want a deeper analytical reading of the text: this requires you to look at the text through some theoretical lens (i.e., that of feminism and gender studies, queer studies, new historicism, the lens of the intertextual and the contextual). Think about what most fascinates you, what most interests you, what stands out as most problematic or troubling in the text. A research paper asks you to step outside the realm of your own analytical reading and step into the realm of discourse.

Entering the discourse means that you explore and research the things you're interested in that other scholars and academic "experts" have been writing about. And then you'll engage or interact with this research, agreeing with some while going against others, all while using their expertise and insight to back up your own research and ideas—we'll get to this a bit later (see Chapter III, Section 3).

Scholars and academics like to write about contextual ideas such as Mary Shelley, a woman, writing about an almost male-exclusive story and world; some like to explore the gender politics in Thomas Malory's

Morte Darthur and potentially what it says about the time period; and some like to understand the philosophical implications Chaucer lays down about religion, the self, the soul, or anything else related to that. In your research, you could come across articles such as:

Aldrich, Marcia and Richard Isomaki. "The Woman Writer as Frankenstein." *Approaches to Teaching Mary Shelley's "Frankenstein."* Ed. Stephen C. Behrendt. New York: MLA, 1990. pp.121–26.

Baldick, Chris. "Tales of Transgression, Fables of Industry: Hoffmann, Hawthorne, Melville, and Gaskell." *Frankenstein's Shadow: Myth, Monstrosity, and Nineteenth-Century Writing.* Oxford: Clarendon Press, 1987.

Triggs, Stephanie. *Congenial Souls: Reading Chaucer from Medieval to Postmodern.* Minneapolis: University of Minnesota Press, 2002.

Collecting Your Research

Before you can actually start engaging with secondary sources, you need to find them. You'll have to take to the Internet and the library to do so. One good place to start is Google or Google Scholar—I repeat, this is a good place to *start*. Google has a habit of spitting out amateur websites, blogs, items related to SparkNotes, and other unofficial or nonauthoritative voices. *Wikipedia* is of course off-limits as a source, but its pages are glutted with informative material and most have an abundance of links to outside sources, academic and official. If you do use *Wikipedia,* use it as a means to seek out official sources.

Just use keywords in your searches: a combination of "Frankenstein" and "feminism" will likely dig up a handful of essays with feminist readings, whereas replacing "feminism" in your search with "queer studies" or "Marxism" will result in entirely different phrases. Just be smart and precise in your keywords. You'll have to begin with a general search, but you'll move to a more specific set of words as you go along.

Relevancy and age is important here. Since many scholars have been working at things for a long time, research and beliefs in each particular field are mutable and open to change. Therefore, you want the most recent scholarly work done in your area of interest: I generally tell my students their articles or books should be no older than ten years.

Most schools will have subscriptions to a number of online academic databases that you can search for articles. You'll have to finagle with your school's electronic library system to access these databases. Good places to scour for research articles include, but are not limited to:

- JSTOR
- Project Muse
- ProQuest Newspapers
- PsycINFO
- PsycARTICLES
- PubMed
- LION: Literature Online
- Arts and Humanities Citation Index

These are just a starter set and barely scratch the surface of available databases. You'll need to figure out what area you'll want to do research (arts and humanities, sciences, social sciences, or psychology, to name a few), and then figure out which databases are best suited for that area of research.

Other places to search would be in **bibliographies** (online or in the back of scholarly books). Bibliographies are **appendixes in the back**

of books or comprehensive lists online that record available scholarly works on particular topics (e.g., there's the *Camelot Project Bibliography* for all things Arthurian, and the massive *Chaucer Bibliography* for academic works related to Geoffrey Chaucer). You can generally take these to be authoritative—whether they're regarded as serious works among fellow scholars is an entirely different thing. Sometimes you'll come across research that no longer holds the same clout or value it once did in the discourse. You can also build on these—if you find an article you really want to work with (either in agreement or disagreement), you can search its own bibliography to find other valuable works it has referenced.

As a sidenote, the upside to searching online databases is that they might sometimes record the number of times a book or article has been cited in other texts. Works that have been cited many times are considered canonical and important scholarly sources—research that has the greatest "expertise" or research that caused major shifts or changes in the scholarship and discourse—that you should glance through if you plan on doing some in-depth work.

Other than online, hitting up the library is also beneficial, since it will most likely have the big books you'll need for your projects. While some articles from books might be online, whole books will be difficult to find; you'll need to consult scholarly books because they cover more material and deeper analytical thought than your typical article.

After collecting your articles and books, it might be a good idea to have everything in one place and organized (I prefer color-coded and alphabetical). If your sources are electronic, and you're able, you might consider printing everything. The benefit to this is there's greater ease in annotating and underlining and leaving marginalia on hardcopy sources than it would be to take notes on your computer or in a separate notebook. Keep yourself organized and get ready to start actually doing the research.

Paper Proposals

For many research papers, instructors will ask for a proposal or abstract, which is a short description (or, since it's submitted in advance, really a prediction) of a full-length paper. Contents need to include the context and specific subject matter or problem and some indication of thesis and methodology—how you're going to carry out your research. Your abstract will usually benefit from a quick list of primary and secondary readings ("such as" is a good word here that lists your research readings, but also leaves room for additional sources). Length varies from one to three paragraphs. Style is more towards the formal.

Even if you're not required to submit a proposal or abstract, if you're going to be writing a paper, drafting up one on your own is a good idea. It's a way to help frame your thoughts; you can also think of the abstract as a primitive outline of your paper and what it's going to entail.

Below is a sample:

Chronological Representations of Merlin:
How the Wizard Earned His Pointy Cap

Many people tend to associate Merlin, perhaps the best-known figure of Arthurian legend after King Arthur himself, with the supernatural and all things magical, typically representing him as a wizard, complete with flowing robes and pointy hat. However, none of these magical attributes are apparent in any early texts concerning Merlin. You won't find him brandishing a wand or topped with a pointy "wizard's" cap in either the original *The History of the Kings of Britain* or Malory's *Morte Darthur*.

My research will trace the chronological appearances of this mysterious figure through the cornerstone texts of Arthurian literature, starting in the 12th century and leading up to the 20th century and beyond—where we see many influences in popular culture—to document the evolution of Merlin's physical appearance, as well as the increasing association with magic.

Key texts include Geoffrey of Monmouth's *The History of the Kings of Britain*, Sir Thomas Malory's *Morte Darthur*, Lord Alfred Tennyson's *Idylls of the King*, and T.H. White's *The Once and Future King*, with special attention to the figure of Merlin and any attributes that might associate him with magic. Along with these cornerstone texts, I will examine a number of other sources, including representations of Merlin in film and the visual arts. I also will consult various secondary sources, such as several of the essays in *Merlin: A Casebook*, a collaboration of works concerning the figure in question by Arthurian experts.

2. The Annotated Bibliography

For all research papers, you will need to include a bibliography (works cited) of all secondary sources consulted. But before you get started with the actual writing, you will need to evaluate and critically engage with your research. For the **annotated bibliography**, you will need to find secondary sources (five to ten is a good place to start) and annotate them. This means you must read and evaluate their worth and relevance in relation to your own paper. In your annotation, you must summarize, assess, and reflect (refer to the example on the next page):

1. **Summarize**: What is the main argument in the source? What is the point of the book or article? What topics are covered? If somebody were to ask you what it is about, what would you say? These are the types of questions that lead the summary. You are not doing any personal reflection or analysis; you are simply summing up the purpose of the academic work.

2. **Assess**: Evaluate the source. Is it useful? Is the information reliable? How does the source evaluate evidence and interact with the text? Is the source making some sort of intervention in the scholarship?

3. **Reflect**: How is this source helpful to you? How does it fit into your own research and argument? Has it changed how you think about your own research?

After completing the annotated bibliography, you should have a good grasp on your research. As such, you should have a strong understanding of where the current scholarship stands in relation to problems you want to raise or tackle in your paper, and you should be able to enter the discourse. You don't need to agree with everything that all your secondary sources say—in fact, if you disagree with something, then that gives you fuel for your own argument. Spend your time countering their claims and coming up with some new way of reading or interpreting something.

Below is a sample annotated bibliography, although not from *Frankenstein*.

Annotated Bibliography Example

Armstrong, Dorsey. *Gender and the Chivalric Community in Malory's Morte d'Arthur*. Gainesville: UP of Florida, 2003.

Dorsey Armstrong's book is a noteworthy source of gender research in Malory's *Morte Darthur*; she claims herself that "a book-length treatment of gender [...] is long overdue" (1), because Malory's work has received mostly cursory attention to gender research. Armstrong examines the function of gender in Malory's *Morte*, and she argues that an understanding of the particular construction of gender in his text is critical to any attempt to engage with its narrative project. Although many commentators claim that Malory's work is "essentially military" and focused on the knights, Armstrong argues against this notion. She claims that the knightly combat and language are actually produced and given meaning by women, thus women are in fact valuable to the formation and stability of the Arthurian society. Armstrong goes on to explore the effects of the Pentecostal Oath, unique only to Malory's work; she claims that it sets up impossible ideals of gender that drive the narrative to its inevitable demise. She states, "In Malory's text, violence and heteronormative gender identity construction concurrently function as both strengths and weaknesses of the courtly social order" (211). These gender ideals are self-destructive, and the source of the downfall of Camelot: these ideals bring about Lancelot's relationship to Guinevere, Gawain's desire for vengeance, and the treacherous Mordred.

In her chapter on Lancelot and Guinevere, Armstrong reads into Lancelot's actions as the flower of chivalry with the lens of Judith Butler. She argues that the narrative of the Morte demonstrates an overwhelming concern with the repetitive performativity of gender; knights must repeatedly go on quests and fights to maintain their masculine knight identity, and ladies must continuously get into trouble for the knights to go rescue them. Malory sets up the Oath, which frames gender boundaries in a juridical power system (which Armstrong turns to Foucault for this); gender, therefore, becomes a pressure point of the community. Armstrong claims that gender is one of the keys to the degenerative progression of the chivalric community, "demonstrating how the idealized knightly devotion to ladies of which chivalric tracts speak may become twisted and warped" (109).

Armstrong's book could prove highly valuable to my own research. My main ideas float around the influences of women in Malory's text. Armstrong notes that he has made several editorial changes to his characters. I want to explore what these changes might say about gender (women specifically) in this chivalric society, and I want to explore what Malory might have been attempting to say about women. Armstrong's insight to the ways gender both constructs and disassembles Arthur's court would be an imperative place to start.

Note: Your annotated bibliography need not be this long, but it should have some depth to it.

3. Engaging with Secondary Sources

Now that you've gone through your secondary sources and annotated them, understanding their position in the discourse and how they help your research, it's time to start interacting with the secondary sources: this is where you enter a discussion and converse with the research.

You should start by organizing the research you agree with: How do these articles or books back you or strengthen your argument? How do their conclusions lead you into the discussion and how do they affect your own reading? These are persuasive authorities: use their expertise to your advantage. Basically you're saying, "If all these people have drawn these similar conclusions from the text, then my argument is strong and worth hearing." Your job is to persuade and convince the reader, to overwhelm them with conviction, and you can accomplish this most by pointing to these authorities. So you make your own claims, and then back them up with textual supports and citations. Here's a good example:

> Studies of women in the *Morte Darthur* have been relatively cursory, such as Dorsey Armstrong remarks, in her book, *Gender and the Chivalric Community in Malory's Morte d'Arthur.*

Your paper is about the treatment of women in Malory's *Morte Darthur* (or insert your favorite piece of literature and topic of research here), and you want to direct the reader to the fact that not much of this has been done. You make your claim, and then you back up your claim with this authoritative voice. Authority gives you strength.

You should avoid cherry-picking in research, meaning don't pick and choose from an academic's work: present their work in its full. It's one thing to indicate you agree with one part of their reading and then disagree with another, but it's something else to just dismiss part of their conclusion and leave it out.

As mentioned before, you want to make counter arguments, particularly in larger research papers: you need to strengthen your own claims and convictions, so you need the space to counter other arguments and explicate on how or why they're wrong and you're right. If Professor A concludes with something you don't agree with, if their conclusion just doesn't seem right, you can go against this with your own **counterclaim**:

> Dorsey Armstrong keenly argues that **X** and **Y**. Where my thoughts diverge from Armstrong's claim is **Y**.

You are allowed to disagree with some authoritative voices if you're not convinced of their evidence, or if your own reading comes to a different conclusion. You make it clear that their work is wrong, in one way or another, and then you must be prepared to offer some rebuttal. You should have very strong evidence that shows both Professor A's conclusions are wrong and also that your conclusions are correct. Persuade your reader.

Evaluating Secondary Sources: Guidelines and Exercise

Remember, your research paper is your own: don't let secondary sources or other authors take over the paper. References and quotations from secondary readings (essays, scholarly articles, academic books, and others) should be used sparingly and only when necessary.

The main source for your argument is your primary source, so your argument and conclusive evidence should be drawn from this reading, not from others' readings. Use secondary readings to help support your thesis and give your paper some authoritative force. Sometimes a critic's work will inspire your own thoughts, and sometimes you will not agree with a critic's work. This is good, but you must present this work in relation to your own reading and interpretation of the text.

The goal is synthesis. Your overall research project will attest to your skill in synthesizing (from the Greek σύνθεσις, a putting together) your thoughts with the authority of your source critics. This should not be a summary of their own research.

Take one of the secondary sources you plan on using for your research:

1. What is the main argument or thesis of this source?

2. How does the critic introduce their evidence? How do they substantiate their claims?

3. Evaluate their own interaction with secondary sources as well as their own critical engagement with the primary source. Does the critic lean more towards one or the other?

4. Do you buy (i.e., accept/agree with) their conclusion? Why or why not?

5. How do you think you could add to the discussion? How can you apply the critic's findings to your own thoughts and ideas?

6. What claims do they make that are particularly topical to your ideas? Think of explicit examples (i.e., quotations) you can reference in your paper.

A general suggestion, really:

After reading each paragraph of the <u>scholarly article</u>, particularly if it gets dense or complex, write the general takeaway or meaning next to each paragraph. Ask yourself: What was the main point of this paragraph? What did I get confused about?

<u>For books</u>: ask yourself the same questions. You might want to write a handy outline of the main ideas of each chapter, and then focus in on particular chapters that are more germane to your final project and topic.

4. Oxford English Dictionary Exercise

Many schools subscribe to a handful of research databases that we consider staples to research. It would be hard to find a school that does not have a subscription to JSTOR—for the liberal arts at least. And the *Oxford English Dictionary* (OED) is another one of those all-important search engines.

The OED is unlike other dictionaries: it will tell you when a word first appeared in English writing and what it meant during that time, be it the 14th, 16th, 18th, or 20th century. For students of English literature and composition, knowledge of, familiarization with, and mastery over the OED's features are invaluable to understanding the mutability of our language. This not only situates you in the linguistic history, but it allows for different (possibly nuanced) meanings of passages you have read before.

On the next page is a set of words first attested to Geoffrey Chaucer: this means that their first appearance in any written manuscript was in Chaucer's work (e.g., *The Canterbury Tales, Troilus and Creseyde, Parliament of Foules*, and others). Your goal in this exercise is to pick <u>three of these words</u> and use the OED to look up its original use, its possible other uses, the citation from Chaucer's work, and the etymology.

universe	dishonest
melancholic	digestion
pharmacy	superstitious
progression	morality
bribe	monster
ecclesiast	chasteness
constant	oppress
elixir	fermentation
annoyance	Milky Way
feminine	magician

For example, we'll work with the word "galaxy."

1. The OED originally defines "galaxy" as a "faintly luminous, irregular band or track encircling the night sky and known to consist of stars,"[1] or in other words the Milky Way. Apparently, over time the word became less specific in meaning and more generally a label for any sort of system that resembled the Milky Way.

2. One of the earliest written accounts comes from Chaucer's *House of Fame*: "Se yonder loo the Galoxie/ Whiche men clepeth the melky weye/ For hit ys white" (l.936)

3. According to the OED, the word comes from the post-classical Latin *galaxias*, from Hellenistic Greek γαλαξίας, from ancient Greek γάλα, meaning "milk." Meaning "galaxy" and "Milky Way" were originally one in the same (the latter being the literal translation of the former), before "galaxy" became a nebulous word for all star systems.

---

1 "galaxy, n." *OED* Online. Oxford University Press, September 2015.

CHAPTER IV

Grammar Grab Bag

Here's where I try to tackle the most common grammatical problems that I have seen in my classroom (they are actually handouts from my class): I'm not going to go through everything that a regular grammar book covers (you can refer to Strunk & White for that). Instead, I've assembled a not nearly comprehensive list of common errors I've found while grading homework, and broken them down into quick reference points. Let's take some time to go over these so that we might learn from our mistakes and better our writing.

1. Common "Whoops"

to vs. too: One of these is a preposition: **to** means toward. It also accompanies verbs to form the infinitive (e.g., **to form**). Too, on the other hand, means "also" or "more than enough." Compare below:

"Lauren is going to the party, and Rachel said she is going **too**."
(Rachel is also going.)

"The winter is **too** cold for Sam." (It is more than enough for him.)
** A trick for this: too has too many O's in it.

---

comparatives and superlatives: We'll be sure to cover these in more detail at a later date. Just remember that when you use a comparative that ends in **-er** (such as **smaller**) OR a superlative in **-est** (e.g., **smallest**), you DO NOT use **more** with it.

Here are some common comparatives and superlatives. These types of adjectives and adverbs tell us to what degree something is; the degrees range from normal to greater (comparative), and the maximum (superlative) degree that something can be.

	Normal	Comparative	Superlative
	sweet	sweeter	sweetest
	tall	taller	tallest
	popular	more popular* less popular*	most popular* least popular*
ex.	"Barry is **more shorter** than Michelle." (wrong) "Barry is **shorter** than Michelle." (CORRECT)		

* use more/less or most/least when the adjective is **more than one syllable**.

---

where/we're/were: This is a similar problem to your/you're and there/their/they're. Compare below, and avoid making these mistakes.

- **Where:** Can be a question word or a relative pronoun: it indicates location. "**Where** is Charles?" "Over there." OR "Charles is over there, **where** he found the football."
- **We're:** Contraction! This means we are, as in "**We're** going to learn these differences."
- **Were:** This is a verb; it is a form of "to be" (e.g., we were, you were, they were).

Once again, **there** is a location word, **they're** is a contraction of they and are, and **their** is the possessive plural pronoun. (e.g., "They're looking for **their** books over *there*.")

Your is the possessive article, and **you're** is a contraction of you and are.
Its is the possessive neuter pronoun, while **it's** is a contraction of it and is.
REMEMBER, an apostrophe does not make plural.

alot: This is not a word; it is **a lot**. Lot means a large amount; therefore, it is a noun that requires an indefinite article ("a"). There is **a lot** of money on the table = there is a large amount of money on the table.

The Comma: The comma (,) is used in a variety of ways. READ and REMEMBER the following ways to use a comma (these are just a few):

1. Separating independent clauses. When you have two main clauses, you can separate them, but **YOU MUST USE** a conjunction: and, but, for, or, nor, so, yet. (Just like I did in this sentence.)

2. Lists of three or more things! "I like apples, oranges, and chocolates."

3. Usually, after introductory words or phrases (e.g., usually, although, while such and such, because, if you do this, *et cetera*).

4. In separating three or more words, phrases, or subordinate clauses. "Yesterday I went to the Apple Store, got some cupcakes at the bakery, and rode the Blue Line."

The Double Negative: Generally* you do not want to write in double negatives. A double negative is when you have two negating signs in a clause (not, no, nothing).

> "We did **not** get **nothing** from the store."

> What you're really saying is, you *did* get something from the store. So, this really doesn't make sense and it doesn't mean what I think you wanted to say. You would need to leave in one of the negative signs. Think about math: when you multiply two negatives, you get a positive.

> * I say generally because there are times when people will write a double negative to add some emphatic umph to their writing, and this is, technically, stylistically correct—the rhetorical term for this is *litotes*. But let's get into the habit of not using these just yet.

Parallelisms: These fancy things are correlative conjunctions that spice up your writing and are cool ways to combine your little sentences into complex ones. Remember, they must always be paired with their counterparts. Always always.

1. **either ... or**: "I **either** want to go to the concert on Friday, **or** to the club on Saturday."

2. **neither ... nor**: "I want to shop at **neither** Banana Republic **nor** Urban Outfitters." This is the negative version of either/or. It would be the same as saying "I do not want to shop at either BR or UO."

   Neither must ALWAYS be paired only with **nor**, and either must ALWAYS go only with **or**.

3. **not only ... but also**: "**Not only** does she want to bake a red velvet cake, **but** she **also** wants to bake a pumpkin pie."

Sentences: Fragments and Run-Ons Cheat Sheet

Run-on sentence: When two independent clauses (two complete sentences) are incorrectly joined.

> ex. "He drove off in the Mercedes Erica watched him go."

Sentence fragment: Phrases or subordinate clauses standing alone. Not a complete sentence with a subject or verb (or required object).

> ex. "Unless you want more coverage than the newspaper story."

Unless what? What is the main idea here? This is actually a subordinate clause and cannot exist without an independent thought/sentence/idea to work with.

How to fix run-on sentences: There are a handful of ways to do so; just make sure your complete thoughts can exist on their own.

1. Use a conjunction. Below is a chart for acceptable conjunctions to help.

Conjunctions	Subordinating Conjunction (for SUBORDINATE clauses only)					
Regular **	Cause/ effect	Compare/ contrast	Place & manner	Possibility and condition	Relation	Time
and, for, or, but, nor, yet, so	because, since, so that	although, even though, though, whereas, while	how, however, where, wherever	if, whether, unless	that, which, who	after, as, before, since, when, whenever, while, until

Usage note: When using a regular conjunction, make sure to pair it with a comma: "He drove off in the Mercedes, **and Erica watched him go."

2. End the sentence with a period and start the next sentence separately.

> ex. "He drove off in the Mercedes. Erica watched him go."

3. Use a semicolon. But what is a semicolon you might ask! Let me tell you about these little guys.

Semicolons join two **COMPLETE** ideas, and **replace** conjunctions. Do not use these with a conjunction; it is not a comma. Read below:

> NO: "He drove off in the Mercedes; **and** Erica watched him go."
> YES: "He drove off in the Mercedes; Erica watched him go."

> They are also used to break up (long) lists that already contain commas: "He went to Rome, Italy; London, England; Moscow, Russia; and Cairo, Egypt."

> Read up on semicolons on http://theoatmeal.com/comics/semicolon.

Other important punctuation, which we will cover in later classes, include the **dash** (—) and **colon** (:); each has a unique use.

Use the **dash** when you want to make an interruption in a sentence to add emphasis. These are standalone punctuation and do not go with commas, semicolons, *et cetera*.

> ex. "She walked in—the tallest woman I'd ever seen *[emphasis!]*—and took a seat at the bar."

> DON'T ADD COMMAS: "She walked in,—the tallest woman I'd ever seen—, and took a seat at the bar."

Use the **<u>colon</u>** to introduce a list. Key words to look for are "as follows" or "following."

> ex. "When he went to the feast, he ate everything: turkey, stuffing, sweet potatoes, green beans, pumpkin pie, pecan pie, and a slice of red velvet cake."

> ALSO use the colon to introduce quotes or an explanation: (like this!)
> Remember this: writing clearly and correctly makes it easier for others to understand.

> "He enjoyed the chocolate fudge cake best: it was rich and very sweet."

2. It's All Relative: Relative Clauses

One problem that students tend to have with their sentence structure is the use of relative clauses. Relative clauses are those that start with W-words (which, who, whom, whose, and that—which isn't a W-word); they have a subject and a verb, but they are subordinate to a previous clause. Now and then, you can think of them as adjective phrases, since they at times add more information. These clauses take the place of nouns or noun phrases when you combine sentences.

- **who:** takes the place of subject-nouns, always people (he, she, we, they)
- **whom:** takes the place of object-nouns, always people (him, her, us, them)
- **whose:** takes the place of possessive pronouns (his, hers, ours, theirs), again . . . always people
- **that:** can take the place of subjects or objects, can refer to people or things, but they must be used when the information is necessary to understanding the sentence

- **which:** takes the place of subjects or objects, but really only refers to things

See for examples:

- Jerry, **who** keeps screwing up in the office, is not well liked among his peers.
- Leslie is very anxious to find out **whom** the public will be voting for.
- Donna, **whose** Mercedes was just cleaned, decided to give nobody a ride.
- Ron is the type of man **that** likes his scotch neat and his bacon plentiful.
- April spent all day at work figuring out **which** dog was her spirit dog.

One slip that students make is separating the clause from its antecedent:

- *Incorrect*: He's going to visit Edinburgh, Scotland. Which is where J.K. Rowling lives.
- *Correct*: He's going to visit Edinburgh, Scotland, which is where J.K. Rowling lives.

If you split the clauses with anything but a comma, you're left with a sentence fragment.

Relative Clause Exercises

Below is a series of exercises for relative clauses and conjunctions (see above). Fill in the blanks with the appropriate relative clauses or conjunctions so that the sentences make sense.

For relative clauses, use who, whom, which, whose, or that.

1. Mark Twain, _____ was an American author, wrote Connecticut Yankee to make fun of the British aristocracy.

2. John did not know to _____ the book belonged, so he asked his friends _____ it was.

3. Dr. Frankenstein read only from very old books, _____ taught him outdated science from ancient alchemists.

4. Dorian Gray grew more and more anxious about the portrait of himself _____ became uglier with every wicked deed.

5. It was Elaine of Astolat _____ gave the red sleeve as a favor to Lancelot.

Conjunction Exercises

Fill in the blanks with the conjunction that best fits.
1. Geoffrey of Monmouth's *Historia* was rather confusing _____ he was more interested in naming all his characters instead of maintaining clear and concise writing.

2. _____ the Arthurian legend was a popular one in the Middle Ages, it didn't get picked up again until the 1800s by Tennyson.

3. Mina wants to know what was in her husband's journal, _____ he came back ill and anxious about the events that happened to him in Transylvania.

4. _____ Arthur was off fighting in France, Lancelot and Guinevere took advantage of his absence for their affair.

5. _____ April couldn't skip class today, she had to finish reading the assigned chapters.

6. Lucy became a vampire _____ Dracula kept biting her.

7. Charles became king, _____ then he made many changes to the country's education system.

Run-on Sentence Worksheet

The following paragraph is muddled by run-on sentences and sentence fragments. Your task in making sense of this information is twofold:

1. Identify run-on sentences (<u>underline once</u>) and correct

2. Identify fragments (<u>underline twice</u>) and correct

The anglerfish is perhaps one of the strangest, most grotesque, and most fascinating fish in the ocean. They can be found up to 3000ft under the ocean they can grow up to 3.3 ft long. The dangling bit is called the esca. Sprouting between its eyes. It's part of the backbone. Some use bioluminescence. With bacteria that collect in the esca. This creates a light that attracts prey to the anglerfish.

For the longest time scientist couldn't find adult male anglerfish sometimes they would notice females would have extra fins. It turns out male anglerfish are many times smaller than the females act as parasites. They fuse. Onto the female anglerfish and their organs dissolve. They essentially become sacs of reproductive organs their sole purpose is to reproduce with females. Female anglerfish can have as many as six male anglers attached to her massive body, they are truly an absurd animal.

The following sentences can either be correct as is, or are examples of run-on sentences (possibly a comma splice). Note if the sentence is correct. If it is not correct, you must correct it by some means: (1) making it two separate sentences; (2) inserting a semicolon; or (3) using a comma and a coordinating conjunction.

1. Both Alexander the Great and Julius Caesar suffered from epilepsy.

2. The Greek playwright Aeschylus was said to have died when an eagle dropped a turtle on his head the eagle mistook his bald head for a rock.

3. Bram Stoker, author of *Dracula* (1897), didn't know about blood types they were discovered in 1901 by Karl Landsteiner he wanted to know why some people died during blood transfusions.

4. One treatment for the Black Death in the 14th century was to place a live hen next to the swelling and drink a glass of your own urine twice a day.

5. The Ancient Egyptian process of mummification involved sticking a long hook up the deceased's nose to break up the brain they would then pull it out.

6. The Ancient Egyptians never removed the hearts during mummification that's where they believed to be the center of intelligence.

7. The months of July and August are named after Julius Caesar and Augustus.

8. Sir Thomas Malory, the author of *Le Morte Darthur*, was arrested for robbery and rape on multiple occasions he then stabbed his way out of prison he swam the moat, meeting up with his gang at Newbold Revel.

9. The French composer Erik Satie only ate things that were white this included eggs, sugar, shredded bones, the fat of dead animals, coconuts, chicken cooked in white water, rice, turnips—just to name a few.

10. Alice Roosevelt, daughter of President Theodore Roosevelt was a rule-breaker she would smoke cigarettes in public (at a time when it was inappropriate) she would stay out late partying she kept a pet snake name Emily Spinach in the White House.

11. In 1887 Nellie Bly faked madness, she got herself thrown into a mental institution in New York City in order to report undercover the abuse and horrendous conditions, this led to outcry and reform.

AFTERWORD

Writing consists of a bunch of old rules, and of course we all know rules were meant to be broken. But the rules can only be broken once you learn them. This is why we have to drill our students on the proper use of the colon and semicolon. It's also why English teachers so adamantly fight their students on the use of "I" or "me" in papers—once you finally learn to distance yourself from paper, then you can break the rule on occasion and slip an "I" in there; once you learn the "rules" of writing, then you will be able to break them as you see fit and find your voice and style in rhetoric.

When I set out to write this book, I never planned a lengthy textbook, nor did I plan for this to be the sole book for the course. For me, as I stated at the beginning of this book, strong writing comes from active engagement with good writing, alongside deep critical thinking. It's never enough to passively retell the plot points or spout back whatever your professor has told you about a text; students should act with curiosity, to look at writing from different angles, to find things they might not have seen before.

Professors are obligated to teach students how to "look" into things, how to ask questions, how to be curious; it isn't enough to teach and grade grammar and "proper" word usage. And it's the student's obligation to actively work with their writing and with their teachers; taking in the teacher's feedback and commentary is the best thing students can do to improve in their writing and critical thinking. I always tell my students, "I can leave as much feedback as you want, but if you don't take the time and effort to read it and see where you need to improve, it does you no good."

As you finish this textbook, you should have a better understanding of the essay in practice: I've been concise, to the point, and brief in my words; I've broken down this paper into the main components and demonstrated how they work both separately and also stitched together. What's most important here is that I've given you the basic tools for writing. It's your job now to take these tools and put in the effort. It's your job now to actively "look" at your own writing and see how the pieces come together as one cohesive body.

FURTHER READING

Writing and Style Guides

Axelrod, Rise B. and Charles R. Cooper. *The St. Martin's Guide to Writing*. 9th ed. Boston: Bedford/St. Martins, 2010.

Gibaldi, Joseph. *MLA Handbook for Writers of Research Papers: 7th Edition*. New York: Modern Language Association, 2009.

Goshgarian, Gary. *Exploring Language*. 14th ed. New York: Pearson Longman, 2014.

Graff, Gerald, Cathy Birkenstein, and Russel K. Durst. *"They Say/I Say": The Moves That Matter in Academic Writing: with Readings*. New York: W. W. Norton & Co, 2012.

Rosenwasser, D. and Stephen, J. *Writing Analytically*. Boston, MA: Thomson Wadsworth, 2006.

Strunk, William, Jr. and E. B. White. *The Elements of Style*. 4th ed. New York: Pearson Longman, 2009.